The Origin and Early History

of

Christianity in Britain

From its Dawn to the Death of Augustine

By

ANDREW GRAY, D.D.

RECTOR OF ST. THOMAS' CHURCH, SOMERVILLE, MASS., AND LECTURER
ON CHURCH HISTORY

With Prefatory Note by

THE RIGHT REV. DR. SEYMOUR

BISHOP OF SPRINGFIELD

"*Ecclesia Britannica ab incunabulis Regia et Apostolica.*"—MONCÆUS

"The British Church was from its cradle Apostolical and Royal"

LONDON

SKEFFINGTON & SON, PICCADILLY, W.

NEW YORK

JAMES POTT & CO., 4TH AVENUE AND 22ND STREET

1897

A REPRINT

PUBLISHED BY

ARTISAN SALES
P.O. BOX 1497 THOUSAND OAKS
CALIF 91360 U.S.A.

ISBN: 0-934666-43-1
LIBRARY OF CONGRESS CATALOG CARD NUMBER: 90-086205

Acknowledgment.

THE Author gratefully acknowledges his obligations to all persons whose works he has in any way laid under contribution in the preparation of the following pages. More especially is he indebted to Rev. R. W. Morgan for valuable aid derived from his " St. Paul in Britain "; to E. J. Newell, M.A., for important extracts from his " Ancient British Church " ; to A. H. Hore, M.A., for the use he has made of his " Eighteen Centuries of the Church in England " ; and to Rev. C. T. Collins Trelawny, M.A., for contributions from " Perranzabuloe, or the Lost Church Found." He trusts that in most cases due credit has been given, and the authorship acknowledged in foot-notes. Where credit has not been so given, it is usually for the reason that the argument has been adapted, but often abbreviated or re-stated, and so is not expressed as in the passage from which it was taken.

Prefatory Note.

Foundations are necessarily out of sight. The beginnings of history are no exception to this rule. Legend, myth and fable often cover them up, and as often the scanty contributions which the makers of nations and pioneer missionaries are able to bequeath to posterity of what they have done, leave their lives and labours in obscurity. Added to this, in rude, rough times there are wars to desolate, and conquests to obliterate, which destroy down to the ground. No ruins even suggest to the beholder that there are crypts beneath.

These reflections come to one when he contemplates the history of Christianity in Britain, prior to the arrival of Augustine, as revealing the foundations on which the splendid and massive superstructure of the Anglican Communion rests.

Augustine began his work *above ground*, or, if not precisely that, he was fortunate in having a sympathizing hand in the Venerable Bede, who industriously preserved a record of his labours and of those of his colleagues and successors, so that what he and his associates and followers wrought and suffered has been kept continuously before the eyes of men.

Beneath Augustinian Christianity in Britain, as well as in Rome, are foundations. Others planted before

Augustine came with his treasures of faith and zeal and self-denial, to build. All honour be to him and his companions, and to the glorious Saint Gregory, who stood behind them with his brave, loving heart, and was their inspiration for their glorious work, but let us not forget those who planted and dropped out of sight in wild, tumultuous, dismal days, when there were few to write, and few to read what was written, and scarcely any to preserve records from the ruthless hand of the destroyer.

The following pages constitute an honest effort to answer this appeal to keep fresh in memory the self-denying labours of missionaries *before Augustine landed in Kent*. The heart of the writer has been in his work, and if his zeal should, in the opinion of any, lead him sometimes to reach conclusions which they think are not warranted by his premises, or to state his deductions with too great assurance of their truth, as though they were ascertained facts of history, still in the main it will be found that the author's purpose has been well worked out, and that he has done a grateful office in uncovering and bringing into view the foundations of the history of the Church of Christ in Britain, and of the Anglican Communion of the present day, thirteen hundred years from the death of St. Columba in Iona in Scotland, and thirteen hundred years from the landing of St. Augustine in Kent, the ecclesiastical home of the Archbishop of Canterbury.

GEORGE F. SEYMOUR,

Bishop of Springfield.

London :
  St. James' Day, 1897.

d

Introduction.

THE *Church of England*, or the " National Church," as she is often called, is probably the *oldest* Institution, ecclesiastical or otherwise, in England. Its history dates back centuries before the time of either State or Monarch. At a period of the Nation's history when there was neither King nor Parliament, the Church was there, the most powerful and flourishing Institution in the land. That Church has played so important a part in the history of the country, in the making of the State itself, that, in the words of Mr. Gladstone, " If we take the Church of England out of the history of England, the history of England becomes a chaos, without order, without life, without meaning." It is of the utmost importance that every man, woman and child, belonging to the Anglican Church, in each and all of its several branches, should know something of the past as well as the present of our dear Mother Church.

The more we learn about the Church and her divine mission, the better we understand the fact that all down the ages of her existence she has stood as a witness for the Truth, the stern opposer of the injustice of cruel kings and crafty potentates, the great promoter of Freedom, the true friend of the poor, and the great educator and benefactor of the people, the more shall

e

we realize what a tremendous power for good the Church
of England exhibits. It has been well said that she
"has not only been a part of the history of the country,
but a part so vital, entering so profoundly into the
entire life and action of the country, that the severing
of the two would leave nothing but a bleeding and
lacerated mass."[1]

Archbishop Benson reminds us[2] that the story of the
Church, "the most interesting, most valuable and most
accessible of studies," is enjoyed by many good Churchmen who never place themselves or their thoughts at
anyone's service. Meanwhile the masses of Church
people are as ignorant of their glorious historic records,
and of the inspiration to be derived from them, as if
they were a sect of yesterday. That it is an unbroken
Church, with unbroken lines of officers and ministers of
peaceful progress, unbroken institutions and usages,
and that it has been and still is the chief "maker of
England" and her greatest civilizer, seldom enters into
the minds of a self-contemplating generation. Yet every
scholar of history knows that the Church of England is
the most precious part of England's heritage, that it
has enriched the land and still enriches it with the best
moral and natural gains. Its doctrine is Scriptural, its
ordinances primitive, its orders Apostolic, its labours
above measure, and its tale is full of

"Words of hope, and bright example given,
    To show through moonless skies that there is light in Heaven."

[1] Mr. Gladstone. Speech in House of Commons, May 16, 1873.
[2] Primary Charge, 1885.

Contents.

The Origin and Early History of Christianity in Britain.

CHAPTER I.

" Ecclesia Anglicana libera sit."—*Magna Charta.*

"ΤΑ ΑΡΧΑΙΑ ΕΘΗ ΚΡΑΤΕΙΤΩ"—*Nic. Council, Can. VI.*

PROPOSITION, THE CASE STATED—EVIDENCE, NATURE OF, ETC.—JOSEPH OF ARIMATHÆA—LAZARUS—DRUIDISM, FAVOURABLE CONDITIONS—CARACTACUS, A CAPTIVE IN ROME—ARISTOBULUS, A MISSIONARY—ST. PAUL IN BRITAIN—EVIDENCE : EUSEBIUS, TERTULLIAN, ORIGEN, ST. JEROME, ST. CHRYSOSTOM, FORTUNATUS THE POET, CLEMENS ROMANUS, THEODORET, GILDAS, ABPS. PARKER AND USHER—TIME AND OPPORTUNITY—INDUCEMENTS : LINUS, CLAUDIA, POMPONIA GRÆCINA—TRIADS OF ST. PAUL—ABBEY OF BANGOR—THE CLOSING SCENE.

THE statement has been made, over and over again, that Christianity was introduced into Britain by St. Augustine and his associates in A.D. 597. It has found its way into the text-books used in our schools, and our children are taught it as authentic history. The impression thus made on the youthful mind is that the Church in England, of pre-reformation times, had its origin entirely from Rome. This most unfounded statement has been repeatedly shown to be utterly untrue to facts, and yet it is accepted by many as correct.

Another false notion, which prevails among Roman Catholics and Protestants alike—and among not a few of the less informed in our own communion also—is that the Church of England was formed or originated at the time of the English Reformation,[1] in the reign of Henry VIII., about A.D. 1534, and that consequently her history extends back only to that date.[2] These statements are so utterly unfounded, that "to assert them is either a confession of gross ignorance or an admission of a deliberate attempt to deceive."

We have no hesitation in saying that "the Christian faith was professed in Britain even in the days of the Apostles, and when the Church of Rome herself was in the feebleness of her infancy. While the Pantheon was yet filled with the multitude of gods, and day by day there ascended the smoke of sacrifice to the Capitoline Jupiter—when Christianity at Rome was recognized only as a 'pernicious superstition,' the adherents to which were doomed to the fire and the stake—even then the name of Christ was honoured on the banks of

---

[1] (a) The word "Reformation" furnishes a refutation. That only can be reformed which already exists.

(b) The Motto of the Reformers is a refutation also : "Let the *ancient* customs prevail."

(c) The first sentence of Magna Charta (A.D. 1215) refutes it : "The *Church of England* shall be free."

[2] See the Author's Pamphlet, "*The Church of England and Henry VIII.,* with introduction by Bishop Seymour." James Pott & Co., New York.

the Thames, and prayers went up to Him in the strange tongue of those on whom Cicero poured his contempt when he wrote to Atticus, and who formed the subject of his jest with Trebatius, when he warned him against a horde of Celtic barbarians." This fact is fully proved by the testimony of ancient writers.

The very early history of the British Church has been involved in some obscurity by the destruction of many of the ancient records; and yet quite enough can be gathered from the history of those remote times to serve our purpose—probably quite as much as can be obtained in support of any contemporaneous event of secular history.

The fairest way probably of treating the subject of the *Introduction* of Christianity into Britain, is to take the statements, often called legendary, see what evidence can be adduced in support of them, and then leave it to the intelligence of the reader to decide how much of truth they contain. The statement will often, necessarily, contain an affirmative proposition. The reader must decide the question, on the evidence furnished, " Are these things so ? "

STATEMENT.

The Statement then is made—and this is a question for the jury to decide—that Christianity was brought into Britain by *Joseph of Arimathæa, circ.* A.D. 36-39; that a little later *Aristobulus* became a Bishop among the Britons; and that *St. Paul* too went there in person. Perhaps also *Simon Zelotes* and others. The first converts are said to have been members of the royal

family of Siluria.[1]   It is asserted that there were too
cradles of Christianity in Britain—"the Chrystal Isle,"
called by the Saxons *Glaston*, in Somersetshire, where
Joseph is believed to have settled and taught; and
Siluria, where Churches and Schools were founded by
the Silurian dynasty.   Glastonbury was commonly
known as Ynys Avàlon, and by the Latins as " Domus
Dei."   Let us now turn to the evidence.

EVIDENCES.

The consecutive evidence in support of this statement
has been collected, at the cost of much research, from
various quarters, and we leave it to all who are
accustomed to examine evidence to decide as to its
value.   But let it be bornc in mind that all historic
evidence must be ruled by times and circumstances.   If
it is such as the times and circumstances of the era
alone admit of, it is entitled to be received in court,
and if there is no contradictory evidence produced to
cancel it, we must ask a verdict of *proven*.   In ages
when literature had but very limited existence, tradition
and general belief are the chief sources to which we
can apply for the essential facts, their details being a
minor consideration.

The constant current of European tradition affirmed
Britain to have been the first country in Europe to

[1] In the year A.D. 36, Bran (or Brennus) resigned the Silurian crown to his
son Caradoc (called by the Latins Caractacus), and became Arch-Druid of the
College of Siluria, where he remained till called to go to Rome as a hostage for
his son.   At the period of his accession Caradoc had three sons, Llyn or
Linus being one of them, and two daughters, Eurgan and Gladys or Claudia.
Vide *St. Paul in Britain*, Morgan, p. 105.

N.B.—In the ancient British language the accent is invariably on the penult receive the Gospel, and the British Church to be the most ancient of all the Churches of Christ therein. The universality of this opinion is readily demonstrated.

1. Polydore Vergil in the reign of Henry VII., and after him *Cardinal Pole* (A.D. 1555), both rigid Roman Catholics, affirmed in Parliament, the latter in his address to Philip and Mary, that "Britain was the first of all countries to receive the Christian faith." "The glory of Britain," remarks Genebrard, "consists not only in this, that she was the first country which, in a national capacity, publicly professed herself Christian, but that she made this confession when the Roman empire itself was pagan and a cruel persecutor of Christianity."

2. This priority of antiquity was only once questioned, and that on political grounds, by the Ambassadors of France and Spain, at the Council of *Pisa*, A.D. 1417. The Council, however, affirmed the British claim. The ambassadors appealed to the Council of Constance (1419) which confirmed the decision of Pisa. It was again confirmed by the Council of Sena, and then assented to. This decision laid down the principle that the Churches of France and Spain were bound to give way, in point of antiquity and precedency, to the Church of Britain, which was founded by Joseph of Arimathæa, "immediately after the passion of Christ."[1]

---

[1] "*Statim post passionem Christi.*" Robert Parsons, the Jesuit, in his *Three Conversions of England*, admits, in common with the great majority of accurate writers, that Christianity came into Britain direct from Jerusalem. " It seems nearest the truth that the British Church was originally planted by Grecian teachers, such as came from the East, and not by Romans." Vol. I., p. 15. The Eastern usages of the British Church alone would attest this fact.

We may therefore accept as the general opinion of Christendom, the priority, in point of antiquity, over all others in Europe, of the British Church. This opinion is well expressed by Sabellius: "Christianity was privately professed elsewhere, but the first nation that proclaimed it as their religion, and called itself Christian after Christ, was Britain."[1]

Gildas, the British historian, who flourished A.D. 520-560, states expressly that the Gospel was introduced into Britain in the last year of Tiberius Cæsar.[2]

The Crucifixion took place in the seventeenth year of Tiberius. The last year would be his twenty-second. Consequently, if we follow Gildas, Christianity was introduced into Britain *five* years after the Crucifixion, that is, A.D. 38.

This is certainly an early period, but Gildas speaks positively, "*ut scimus*." And this date synchronizes

---

[1] Sabell. *Enno*, lib. vii., c. 5.

[2] "We know that Christ, the true Sun, afforded His light to our island in the last year of Tiberius Cæsar." "*Tempore ut scimus, summo Tiberii Cæsaris.*" *Histor. Briton.* Usher terms Gildas "*auctor veracissimus.*"

"De Britanica Ecclesia nostra liquidum est fuisse eam aliquot *ante* Romanam *annis* fundatam . . . . *Glaciali* (inquit Gildas) frigore vigenti insulæ (de Britannia agit) Christus suos radios, id est sua præcepta, indulget, tempore ut scimus summo Tiberii Cæsaris. Supremum Tiberii tempus incidit in XVII. kal. April A.D. XXXIX. natalitia vero *Romanæ Ecclesiæ* in XV. kal. Feb. A.D. XLV. (Teste Baronio). Disce jam hinc sapere disce Romanam Ecclesiam Britannicæ nostra non *matrem* sed *sororem* atque *sororem* integro quinquennio *minorem.*" (Ex Crakenthorpe, *Defensio Eccl. Angl.* p. 23.)

TRANSLATION.

"Of our British Church it is certain that it was established several years before the Roman . . . . Christ (says Gildas) granted His rays, that is His precepts to this island (he is speaking of Britain) then numb with glacial cold, as we know in the last year of Tiberius Cæsar. The last year of Tiberius Cæsar fell on the XVII. kal. April A.D. 39. The birth of the Roman Church being (according to Baronius) on the XV. kal. Feb. A.D. 45. Now learn to know from this, learn (I say) that the Roman Church is not the mother of our British Church, but the sister and a sister the younger by five whole years."

with the first persecution of the Church by Saul of Tarsus, and the subsequent and general dispersion. "They were all scattered abroad except the Apostles."[1] And if "*all*," then Joseph of Arimathæa among them. Regarding this date (given by Gildas) as our starting point, we have several testimonies assigning the first introduction of Christianity in or about the same year to *Joseph of Arimathæa.*

1. Maelgwyn of Llandaff, the uncle of St. David, writing about A.D. 450, says: " Joseph of Arimathæa, the noble decurion, received his everlasting rest with his eleven associates in the Isle of Avàlon. He lies in the Southern angle of the (bifurcated line of the) Oratorium of the adorable Virgin."[2] This is British testimony from one who was personally acquainted with the interior of the Church at Avàlon (Glastonbury), the " Domus Dei," and knew the exact spot where Joseph is said to be buried.[3] The greater weight is due to this evidence of Maelgwyn's, as no fact is better established than the reconstruction of the *Domus Dei* on a cathedral scale by his nephew, St. David.

[1] Acts viii. 1.

[2] Thick Vellum Cottonian MS. quoted also by Usher, *Melchini Fragmentum*, vide *St. Paul in Britain*, Morgan, p. 139. Joseph of Arimathæa is by Eastern tradition said to have been the younger brother of the father of the Virgin Mary.

[3] "The Church at Glastonbury, from its antiquity called by the Angles the 'Ealde Church,' savoured of sanctity from its very foundation." . . . "There is no corner of the church in which the ashes of some saint do not repose. The very floor, inlaid with polished stones, and the sides of the altar itself, above and beneath, are laden with a multitude of relics. The antiquity, and the multitude of saints buried there, have endowed the place with such sanctity that at night scarcely any one presumes to keep vigil there, or during the day to spit upon the floor. St. David, that celebrated, incomparable man, built and dedicated the second Church here, and here his remains repose." *William of Malmsbury*, Book I., c. 2. St. Aidan, too, was buried by the side of St. David.

2. The Vatican MS. quoted by Baronius in his "Ecclesiastical Annals," *ad annum* 35,—the same year in which the Acts of the Apostles state that "all except the Apostles were scattered abroad"—records that (in this year) Lazarus, Mary, Martha, Magdalene, Marcella their servant, Maximin a disciple, St. Philip, and Joseph of Arimathæa, against all of whom the Jews had special enmity, were banished from Judea and exposed to the sea in a vessel without sails or oars. The vessel drifted many days in the Mediterranean, being tossed by storms hither and thither, but ultimately arrived safely at Marseilles. St. Philip remaining in those parts, sent Joseph with a few companions into Britain to preach the Gospel there and convert the Britons to the Faith. On their arrival they were hospitably received by Arviragus,[1] the king of that portion of the country where they landed. He gave them the island then called Ynys Wydrin or Ynys Avàlon, now Glastonbury. Here they built a small Church of "hurdle-work," and "here they watched, prayed, fasted, preached," converting many to the Christian Faith, "having *high* meditations under a *low* roof, and large hearts betwixt narrow walls."[2] Here, too, Joseph and his companions lived and died, and here they were buried.[3]

3. The "Chronicon" of Pseudo-Dexter and the

---

[1] "*Regem aliquem capies, aut de tempore Britanno excidet Arviragus.*" (Juvenal, Sat. iv. 126.)

[2] Fuller, Book I., Sec. i. 11-13.

[3] The respective dates, 35 and 38, allow of three years between the expulsion of Joseph from Judea and his settlement in Britain, an undesigned harmony which goes far chronologically to confirm the common record.

Fragmenta of Haleca, Archbishop of Saragossa, furnish the same statement, professedly from primitive sources of unknown date. Cressy, Sanders, and Alford, all Roman Catholic historians, concur with Gildas as to the year, and with the authorities already quoted in regard to the statement that Joseph of Arimathæa was the first to preach the Gospel in Britain.

4. We possess evidence that Churches were erected in Britain before the close of the second century, and whatever direction our investigations take, we find authority for the statement that the Church of Joseph of Avàlon, or Glastonbury, was the first and oldest of them all, many affirming that it was the oldest or senior Church in *the whole world*.

It will be interesting to give the conclusions arrived at by a few of .the historians who have treated this subject.

" The Church of Avàlon, in Britain, no other hands than those of the disciples of the Lord themselves built." *Publius Discipulus*.

" The mother Church of the British Isles is the Church in Insula Avallonia, called by the Saxons Glaston." *Usher*.

" If credit be given to ancient authors, this Church of Glastonbury is the senior Church of the world." *Fuller*.

" It is certain that Britain received the faith in the first age from the first sowers of the Word." *Sir Henry Spelman*.

Had any doubt existed, on this point of priority, it certainly would have been contested by some of the other Churches, for it was not a mere question of chronology, but one which carried with it enormous privileges and advantages. It was universally conceded, however, and upon it the long series of royal charters of the Church and Monastery, from that of King Arthur, the nephew of its second founder, St. David, to that of Edward III. proceeded. "The first Church in the kingdom, built by the disciples of Christ," says the charter of Edgar. "This is the city," states the charter of Ina, "which was the fountain and origin of Christ's religion in Britain, built by Christ's disciples." The tombs of British and Saxon kings, saints, bishops, and abbots buried in and around it confirm the charters.

Of the general truth of the Arimathæan mission there have been numerous supporters. No author, indeed, who had taken pains to examine its evidence, rejects its main facts. "We dare not deny," says *Fuller*, "the substance of the story." *Bishop Godwin*, in his quaint style, writes, "The testimonies of Joseph of Arimathæa's coming here are so many, so clear, and so pregnant, that an indifferent man cannot but discern that there is something in it." *Archbishop Usher* defends it with his usual display of erudition, and with unusual vehemency of manner, as if the honour of ecclesiastical Britain rested on its truth. And it is well known that *Archbishop Parker*, in his letter to Calvin, concerning the proposal of a union among all Protestants, reminds him that the Church of England would "retain her Episcopacy ; but not as from Pope Gregory, who sent Augustine the monk hither, but from Joseph of Arimathæa." [1]

---

[1] Strype's "Archbishop Parker," Vol. I., p. 139.

We reject, of course, the addenda and crescenda, the legends and marvels, which, in after ages, monks and historians piled high and gorgeously on the original foundation. That foundation, however, must have possessed no mean strength, depth, and solidity, to bear the immense superstructure which mediæval superstition and literature erected over the simple tomb of the Arimathæan senator in the Isle of Avàlon.

Leaving details out of the question, the cardinal features of the mission of Joseph of Arimathæa into Britain are entitled to acceptance. These features may be regarded as the following :—

Joseph and his companions (*vide* p. 8) came from Marseilles into Britain about A.D. 36-39, and located at Ynys Avàlon, the seat of a Druidic Cor, which was subsequently made over to them in *free gift by Arviragus*. Here they built the first church, which became the centre and mother of Christianity in Britain. Here, too, they (or several of them) terminated their mortal career. The gentle and conciliatory character of Joseph secured the protection of the reigning family and the conversion of some of its members. Joseph died and was interred here, A.D. 76. His tomb was inscribed with the following epitaph, touching by its spirit of faith, peace, and humility : " *Ad Britannos veni post Christum Sepelivi. Docui Quievi.*" After A.D. 35-36 Joseph disappears from the Scripture narrative.

The Greek and Roman martyrologies and menologies commemorate with scrupulous jealousy the obituaries and death-places of all the earlier Christian characters of mark who died within the pale of the Roman empire.

They nowhere record that of Joseph. Now we know from Tertullian that Britain was Christian before it was Roman. The dove conquered where the eagle could not penetrate. " Regions in Britain which have never been penetrated by the Romans," he says, " have been subdued to Christ." If this statement was correct, after the war between Rome and Britain had been carried on for a century and a half, from A.D. 43 to 192 —and in a national point of view the testimony is impartial, for Tertullian was an African—it is obvious that the mission of Joseph must have been founded in the very heart of independent Britain, quite out of the pale, therefore, of the Roman empire. And this inference tallies with the rest of the evidence. Joseph died in these " *loca inaccessa Romanis.*" His death, therefore, would not be chronicled by Greek or Roman Churches.

LAZARUS.

Lazarus is said to have accompanied Joseph. The only record we possess of him, beyond the Scripture narrative,[1] is in a very ancient British Triad : " The Triad of Lazarus, the three councils of Lazarus: Believe in God Who made thee ; Love God Who saved thee ; Fear God Who will judge thee." It is difficult to explain how the name and council of Lazarus could find their way into these peculiarly British memorials except by his presence and teaching in Britain.

DRUIDISM.

The Druidic religion knew no such thing as *intolerance*

---

[1] The tradition of the Church at Lyons is that he returned with Martha and Mary to Marseilles, of which town he became the first Bishop, and died there.

and persecution. There is no instance of Druidism persecuting conscience or knowledge. Such a condition of things was left for Rome, for a religion of foreign importation. Whatever the errors of Druidism were, it possessed some grand features. Its foundation maxim was, "*Truth against the world.*" St. Paul's maxim, "*We can do nothing against the truth,*" breathes a kindred spirit, and would at once conciliate a Druidic hearer.

Now if we cast one eye on Britain, on a Druidic Caractacus, Arviragus, or Claudia, listening from their thrones to a Christian missionary because he professed to bring and to preach the truth, and Christ as the Truth, the Way, and the Life ; then cast the other on a Pilate, asking in the profoundest disbelief in all virtue and goodness, "What is truth ? " we shall see at a glance that Britain was prepared, and the Roman empire was not prepared, for Christianity. The British and the Roman minds were different. Druidism, therefore, dissolved by the natural action of its own principles into Christianity. No persecution until the tenth, under Diocletian, reached Britain ; for Christianity had become nationality. And the Diocletian persecution was stopped in two years by Constantius, on his own responsibility, at the hazard of a civil war. Then rose Constantine with an army determined to put a stop to the persecution of Christianity everywhere. The clue is a national, a British one.

> " Truth crushed to earth shall rise again,
> The eternal years of God are hers ;
> But error, wounded, writhes in pain,
> And dies amid her worshippers. '

CARACTACUS.

From those valuable historical documents, the Welsh Triads—written originally in the British dialect—it appears that Caràdoc (Caractacus) was betrayed and delivered up to the Roman Commander by Arègwedd, about A.D. 51, and taken to Rome. Brân (Brennus) his father, Llyn (Linus) his son, Eurgan a daughter, and Gladys (Claudia) a second daughter, were all taken to Rome likewise, and there detained seven years as hostages for Caractacus.

Tacitus furnishes an account of the battle which terminated the career of Caràdoc in field. Caràdoc seeing that the Romans were victorious, and that his own wife and daughter had fallen into the hands of the conquerors, took refuge himself, at her repeated solicitations, at Caer Evroc (York), with Arègwedd, Queen of the Brigantes, and grand-niece of the infamous traitor in the Julian war, Mandubratius or Avarwy. Here by her orders, with hereditary treachery, he was seized while asleep in her palace, loaded with fetters, and delivered to Ostorius Scapula. On receiving intelligence of the event, Claudius ordered him and all the captive family to be sent to Rome. The approach and arrival of Caràdoc at Rome are finely described by the ancient historians—"*Roma catenatum tremuit spectare Britannum*" —Rome trembled when she saw the Briton, though fast in chains.

The Senate was convened and the trial of Caràdoc began. With an unaltered countenance, the hero of forty battles, great in arms, greater in chains, took his position before the Emperor and defended himself in the following utterances:

"Had my government in Britain been directed solely with a view to the preservation of my hereditary domains or the aggrandizement of my own family, I might long since have entered this city an ally, not a prisoner; nor would you have disdained for a friend a king descended from illustrious ancestors and the director of many nations. My present condition, stript of its former majesty, is as adverse to myself as it is a cause of triumph to you. What then? I was lord of men, horses, arms, wealth: what wonder if at your dictation I refused to resign them? Does it follow, that because the Romans aspire to universal dominion, every nation is to accept the vassalage they would impose? I am now in your power—betrayed, not conquered. Had I, like others, yielded without resistance, where would have been the name of Caràdoc? Where your glory? Oblivion would have buried both in the same tomb. Bid me live, I shall survive for ever in history one example at least of Roman clemency."

Such an address as this, worthy a king, a soldier, and a freeman, had never before been delivered in the Roman Senate. Tacitus thought it worthy to be reported and immortalized by his pen. The preservation of Caràdoc forms a solitary exception in the long catalogue of victims to the policy then in vogue; nor can it be accounted for, considering the inflexibility of Roman military usage, in any other way than by an immediate and supernatural intervention of providence, which was leading by the hand, to the very palace of the British king at Rome, the great Apostle of the Gentiles. The family of Aulus Plautius—a lieutenant in the army of Claudius—was already connected with that of Caràdoc, he having married Gladys ("Pomponia Græcina"), the sister of Caràdoc. Besides, an engagement existed between Gladys (Claudia), the daughter of Caràdoc, and Rufus Pudens Pudentinus, a young Roman Senator of large possessions. But their united influence would not have sufficed to alter a fixed law of the Roman state in favour of an enemy who had tasked its uttermost powers and resources for so many years. " In Britain," says Tacitus, " after the captivity of Caractacus, the Romans were repeatedly conquered and put to the rout by the Silures alone." Perhaps this knowledge, and a feeling that the execution of Caràdoc might still further imperil the Roman states in Britain, together with the consideration that clemency might be the wisest policy towards a high-spirited and royal enemy, dictated the course of Claudius. But, be this as it may, *the life of Caràdoc was spared*, on condition of his never again bearing arms against Rome. A residence of *seven years* in free custody ("*libera custodia*") at Rome was imposed upon him. His father Brân was accepted as one of his hostages, and he was allowed the full enjoyment of the revenues of his Silurian domains, which were forwarded to him by his subjects and council. Gladys his daughter was adopted by the Emperor Claudius, and took his family name Claudia. Caràdoc took up his residence in the *Palatium Britanni-cum*, on the Mons Sacer, converted afterwards by his grand-daughter Claudia Pudentiana into the *first Christian Church at Rome*, known first as the "*Titulus*," and now as the Church of *St. Pudentiana*.[1] Here the nuptials of Claudia and Rufus Pudens Pudentinus were celebrated A.D. 53. Four children were the issue of this marriage—St. Timotheus, St. Novatus, St. Pudentiana, and St. Praxedes. Of the sons of Caràdoc, Cyllinus and Cynon returned to Britain, the former succeeding on his father's death to the Silurian throne. The second son Llyn (Linus) remained with his father, and was, as we shall see subsequently, consecrated probably by St. Peter and St. Paul, *first Bishop of Rome*.

The attachment between Pudens and Claudia first began when the former was stationed by Aulus Plautius (as prætor castrorum) at Regnum, now Chichester. There is in the Chichester Museum a very interesting monument of the residence of Pudens in that city. *Cogidunus*, regulus of the Regni, was one of the kings included as allies—in fact, tributaries—under the Roman protectorate in the Claudian treaty of Colchester. Tacitus remembered him, as he well might. For Tacitus was born A.D. 56, the year after the death of Claudius, and Cogidunus was still alive A.D. 76, some ten years after the martyrdom of St. Paul, when Tacitus was in his twentieth year. In A.D. 1723, whilst excavating for the foundation of some houses, the monument, to which we refer, generally known as the *Chichester Stone*, was discovered. The inscription, which was partly mutilated, and is cut in very bold characters, as restored by Horsley and Gale, is as follows :—

[1] I had the pleasure of visiting this interesting spot when in Rome in July, 1888.

" Neptuno et Minervae
Templum
Pro Salute Domus Divinae
Ex Auctoritate Tib: Claudii
Cogiduni Regis Legati Augusti in Britannia
Collegium Fabrorum et qui in eo
A sacris sunt de suo dedicaverunt
Donante Arcam Pudente Pudentini Filio."

Translation.—" The College of Engineers, and ministers of religion attached to it, by permission of Tiberius Claudius Cogidunus, the king, legate of Augustus in Britain, have dedicated at their own expense, in honour of the divine family (the imperial family) this temple to Neptune and Minerva. The site was given by Pudens, son of Pudentinus."   The temple was erected about A.D. 50, before the conversion of Pudens, and before his marriage with Claudia.

We have now (A.D. 56) the royal Silurian family at Rome, in the *Palatium Britannicum* on the Mons Sacer. This palace was afterwards called the " Titulus " or " Hospitium Apostolorum," and later " *St. Pudentiana*," which name the building still retains.   The minister of this Church, and Chaplain of the family of Pudens, was most likely Hermas, mentioned by St. Paul,[1] and sur-named, from his work bearing the title of *Pastor*, Hermas Pastor.   After him the Church was also called Pastor. In front of this relic of eminent British and Apostolic times may be seen, carved in characters corroded by age, the Latin inscription, attributed to the second century, of which the following is a translation :—

" In this sacred and most ancient of Churches, known as that of Pastor, dedicated by Sanctus Pius Papa, formerly the house of Sanctus Pudens, the senator, and

[1] Rom. xvi. 14.

the home of the holy Apostles, repose the remains of three thousand blessed martyrs, which Pudentiana and Praxedes, Virgins of Christ, with their own hands interred."[1] *Baronius* has the following note on the Titulus: "It is delivered to us by the firm tradition of our forefathers that the house of Pudens was the first that entertained SS. Peter and Paul, and that there the Christians assembling formed the Church, and that of all our Churches (at Rome) the oldest is that which is called after the name of Pudens."[2]

While at the Palatium Britannicum, Brân, probably Caràdoc, certainly Linus and Claudia, became converts to Christianity; if, indeed, the two last named had not previously espoused the Christian Faith, and now "learned the way of God more perfectly." Now let it be remembered that St. Paul, as Jerome states, was sent to Rome "in the second year of Nero," *i.e.*, A.D. 56,[3] and remained there a prisoner at large for *two years*. This was the first time St. Paul had ever seen Rome, on his appeal to Cæsar. They were all released at the same time, A.D. 58. Here, then, is a coincidence worthy

[1] Adjacent to the palace were baths on a corresponding scale. These baths and grounds were bequeathed by Timotheus to the Church at Rome, and they were the only buildings and grounds of any magnitude possessed by the Roman Church till the reign of Constantine. This *Titulus* was the *hospitium* for Christians from all parts of the world.

[2] *Annales Ecclesias*, in Notis ad 19 Maii. *Vide* also Moncæus' *Syntagma de Claudia Britannica*, p. 18; Pastoris Epistolæ ad Timotheum; Justini Martyris Apologia; Greek Menology, ad dies Pudentianæ et Praxedis.

That the palace of Claudia was the home of the Apostles in Rome appears agreed upon by all Ecclesiastical historians. Even Robert Parsons, the Jesuit, admits it. "Claudia was the first hostess or harbourer of St. Peter and St. Paul at the time of their coming to Rome." *Three Conversions of England*, Vol. I., p. 16.

[3] With this date agree Bede, Cave, Stillingfleet, Alford, Godwin, *De Præsulibus*, Rapin, Bingham, Stanhope, Warner, Trapp, and others.

of note between the detention of these British person-
ages, and that of St. Paul at Rome. And it is most
reasonable to infer that it was through the instrumentality of that Great Apostle to the Gentiles that the
British captive, Caractacus, and the hostages before
named, or several of them, embraced Christianity.

We are now prepared to consider the question of *St.
Paul's Mission to Britain,* and his connection with the
Church there.

ARISTOBULUS AND ST. PAUL IN BRITAIN.

" When Brân was set at liberty "—which we have
already seen was in A.D. 58—"he returned to Britain,
taking with him *three* other converts to Christianity.
One of these was Ilid, a converted Jew, another Cyndaf,
and the third (Arwystli), appears to have been that very
Aristobulus whose 'household' was saluted by St. Paul,
in his Epistle to the Romans, at the beginning of the
same year." [1]

This conclusion is greatly strengthened from the
fact that *Nicephorus,* a Greek historian, and another
Greek author, *Dorotheus,* both record that Aristobulus
went into Britain, that he was consecrated by St. Paul
the first Bishop of that Church, that he made many
converts, ordained Priests and Deacons, and finally
died there. [2] " It is perfectly certain," writes Alford, [3]
" that before St. Paul had come to Rome Aristobulus

[1] *Welsh Triads.*

[2] These authorities are quoted at length in Usher, *Primordia,* pp. 9, 744,
745, and several others added. Aristobulus is also described in the Greek
Martyrologies and in the " Genealogy of the Saints," originally written in the
British language as the first Bishop of the Britons.

[3] Alford's *Regia Fides,* Vol. I., p. 83. A work of much erudition.

was absent in Britain." The most reasonable conclusion is that Aristobulus, who was a Greek, was
commissioned by St. Paul in the East. That he
brought his "household" with him as far as Rome
and left them there. That while there he made the
acquaintance of the British family at the Palatium
Britannicum, and that he went on to Britain *shortly
before the British captive.* Be this as it may, however,
there appears to be sufficient evidence that Aristobulus
did preach the Gospel in Britain, and that he finally
died there.

The Martyrologies of the Greek Church record that :
" Aristobulus was one of the seventy disciples and a
follower of St. Paul, along with whom he preached the
Gospel and ministered to him. He was chosen by St.
Paul to be the Missionary Bishop to the land of
Britain, inhabited by a fierce and warlike race . . .
There he built Churches and ordained deacons and
priests for the Island."

Haleca, to the same effect, says : " The memory of
the martyrs is celebrated by the Britons, especially
that of Aristobulus, one of the seventy disciples."[1]
Dorotheus (A.D. 303) : " Aristobulus, who is mentioned
by St. Paul in his Epistle to the Romans, was made
Bishop of Britain." [2]

The " Genealogies of the Saints " of Britain say :
" These came with Brân the Blessed from Rome to
Britain—Arwystli Hên (Senix), Ilid, Cyndaf, men of
Israel ; and Maw or Manaw, son of Arwystli Hên."

[1] Haleca, Bishop of Augusta, *Fragmenta in Martyr.*

[2] *Synopsis ad Aristobulum.*

Now according to the genius of the British dialect Arwystli becomes Aristobulus.

A district in Montgomeryshire, on the Severn, perpetuates by its name (" Arwystli ") the scene of his martyrdom.

The Britons must have had Arwystli among them in person, and been struck by the age of the venerable missionary, or the epithet *Senex* (Hên) would not have become amongst them part of his name.[1]

ST. PAUL IN BRITAIN.

St. Paul, who travelled extensively, and mixed with all classes of society, must have been as well acquainted with Britain and the events transpiring there, as any other intelligent citizen. There was much to attract him to Britain as a field of Gospel labour and enterprise. We know from Scripture evidence that he contemplated a journey to Western Europe. A reference to the Epistle to the Romans (xv. 24, 28), shows that his journey to Spain was meditated not only before he came to Rome, but also that it was the principal object of his leaving the East. " Whensoever I take my journey into Spain, I will come to you, for I trust to see you on my journey, and to be brought on my way thitherward by you." He speaks of the journey as a thing decided upon, and that he intended making Rome a stage in that journey, and deriving advantage in the prosecution of it, from the help he expected from that place. All

[1] Aristobulus must have been advanced in years, for he was, it is said, father-in-law of St. Peter. His wife was probably the subject of the miracle recorded by St. Matthew. His daughter bore St. Peter a son and a daughter. *St. Paul in Britain*, Morgan, p. 153.

the incidents and delays which occurred between this date (A.D. 56), and the termination of his first imprisonment, were interruptions of his original plan of operations. His destination was the far West in accordance with the words of Christ, " I will send thee *far* hence to the Gentiles." At Rome, then, he abode two whole years, preaching the Kingdom of God and teaching those things which concern the Lord Jesus Christ with all confidence ; the things which had happened to him falling out to the furtherance of the Gospel; his bonds in Christ being manifest in the Palace and in all other places.[1]

The Acts of the Apostles embrace only so much of his history as ends with his first imprisonment at Rome; but there remains at least five or six years—the time between his liberation from that first imprisonment, and the date of his second imprisonment and martyrdom—to be accounted for. It cannot be supposed that he was taking his ease during such an interval. The energy of his character, the sense of his responsibility, and the spiritual wants of the world, alike forbade it: He is now actually in Rome, though brought there under circumstances which he could not have foreseen when he penned the Epistle to the Romans. He is at Rome, and at liberty, and the wide world once more before him. What more probable than that he should profit by the occasion now afforded him, of completing his plan—his tendency still Westward from the very beginning of his ministry—and go forwards into Spain and Britain ? We think we are justified in

---

[1] Phil. i. 12, 13.

the conclusion that having already, as has been before
stated, sent Aristobulus into Britain a short time before,
he would carry out his purpose of visiting Spain, and
would then join his fellow-labourer in Britain ; for it is
plain that Aristobulus acted as much under his instructions in Britain as Titus in Crete or Timothy in
Ephesus.

Gades, in Spain, now Cadiz, was no doubt the place
which St. Paul had especially in mind when he wrote
of his intended journey.   It was at that time the
commercial centre of Western Europe, the capital of
the district of Boetica, and the old Tarshish of
Scripture.[1]   Not only was it a great commercial centre,
but one of the routes of communication *between
Rome and Britain was via Gades ;* so that any one
at Gades would find ample opportunity of going to
Britain in one of the crafts that plied between the
two countries.

The conclusion generally arrived at by writers who
have investigated this subject may be given in the
words of Capellus : " I scarcely know of one author,
from the times of the Fathers downwards, who does
not maintain that St. Paul, after his liberation, preached
in every country in Western Europe, Britain included."
The same opinion substantially is held by Baronius,
and also by Griffith or " Alford," next to Baronius the
most erudite of Roman Catholic historians ; and by
Archbishops Parker and Usher, Stillingfleet, Camden,
Gibson, Cave, Nelson, and others.   Both St. Chrysostom
and Theodoret assert, without any hesitation, in so

1 *The Anglican Church*, R. H. Cole, B.D., pp. 14, 15.

many words, that to Spain the Apostle went after his imprisonment at Rome.[1] Indeed Theodoret says "to Spain and other nations, *and to the islands lying apart in the ocean.*" St. Jerome affirms that after his first imprisonment he preached the Gospel in Spain. And to cite one more writer on this point, Bishop Wordsworth, of Lincoln, says : "We find clear testimony, dating from St. Paul's age, that the Apostle, who in his first confinement was at Rome for the first time, and had never reached any point beyond it, did not terminate his career there *at that time*, but went to some regions *westward* of Rome."[2] It may fairly be presumed that these witnesses furnish sufficient evidence to prove that St. Paul did carry out his intention of "taking a journey into Spain." We will now summon other witnesses, who, with those already heard, will show that he went not to Spain only, but also to Britain.

Eusebius, when showing that the Apostles "preached their doctrines in the remotest cities and countries," particularly adds "that some passed over the ocean to those which are called the British islands."

Tertullian (A.D. 190), says : "There are places in Britain inaccessible to the Romans which have been subdued to Christ."[3]

Origen (A.D. 230), says : "The power of God our Saviour is ever with them in Britain who are separated from the world."

St. Jerome (A.D. about 400), says that St. Paul's

[1] Pearson, *Minor Theological Works*, I., p. 392.

[2] *New Testament with Notes*, Introduction to Epistles to Timothy and Titus, p. 429.

[3] "Loca inaccessa Romanis."

preaching extended "as far as the earth itself," and that he "preached the Gospel in the Western parts."[1]

St. Chrysostom (about A.D. 400), in his eloquent comparison of St. Paul with Nero, in the fourth Homily on 2 Timothy, speaks of the former as having been "known and honoured by the world, and by those of the extreme limit of the world."[2] Again, he says, "The British islands, situated beyond our sea and lying in the very ocean, have felt the power of the Word, for even there churches are built and altars erected."

Venantius Fortunatus, the poet (A.D. 500), says that St. Paul having "crossed the sea to Great Britain, reached Thule and the ends of the earth."[3]

Clement of Rome, a contemporary of St. Paul, whom that Apostle calls his "fellow labourer" and says that his "name is in the book of life,"[4] had ample opportunities of conversing with him and being familiar with his journeys. He was Bishop of Rome, and wrote Epistles from that city to the Corinthians, about A.D. 87, some twenty years after the martyrdom of St. Paul, "whilst he had," as St. Irenæus says, "the preaching of the Blessed Apostles still ringing in his ears, and their traditions before his eyes." In them he describes St. Paul's labours and sufferings with great minuteness. He speaks of his having "become the

---

[1] *Catal. Eccl. Script.* 9.   Hore, p. 14, note.

[2] St. Chrysostom, Hom. IV., on 2 Tim. iv. 10. "The name of the one the greater part of the people have not heard of (Nero). The other is daily celebrated by Greeks and Barbarians, Scythians, and those who inhabit the extremities of the earth."

[3] Lib. iii. *De Vita S. Martini*, quoted by Fuller, Book I., Cent. i., § 1, 8 ; also by Hore, p. 14, note.

[4] Phil. iv. 3.

herald of God in the East and in the West; of his having preached Righteousness to the whole world, and having come to the *extreme limit of the West*"—καὶ ἐπὶ τὸ τέρμα τῆς δύσεως.[1] He speaks of his "preaching as far as the extremity of the earth" and "preaching the Gospel in the Western parts"—expressions which Bishop Stillingfleet has fully shown must have been used with reference to Britain. Clement, being a man of Greek culture, and writing from Rome in an age when Gaul, and Spain, and Britain had been opened out by the Roman arms, and had been made subject to Rome, would give a very definite meaning to the phrase "*the extreme limits of the West.*" Plato uses the phrase in a limited sense; but Plato knew nothing of the conquest of Britain and of its civilization by Rome, as Clement did. So we must look to other writers for the meaning of Clement's term. Roman Colonies were planted in Britain at an early period of the Conquest, and these would, naturally, be the "limits of the West," to a man writing from Rome. Horace supports this. He speaks of the Britons as "*ultimos orbis Britannos.*"[2] So, too, Catullus, "*ultimos Britannos.*" Herodotus, many centuries before, described the "Celts" of Gaul

---

[1] The passage *in extenso* runs thus: "St. Paul, having seven times worn chains, and been hunted and stoned, received the prize of such endurance. For he was the herald of the Gospel in the West as well as in the East, and enjoyed the illustrious reputation of the faith, in teaching the whole world to be righteous. For after he had been to the extremity of the West, he suffered martyrdom before the sovereigns of mankind; and thus, delivered from the world, he went to his holy place, the most brilliant example of steadfastness that we possess." Clem. Rom. *Epistola Corinthios*, c. 5.

[2] *Od.* i. 35. Serves iturum Cæsarem in ult, etc. Catullus (B.C. 48), Lib. Veron. Car. XI., "horribilesque ultimosque Brit." Quoted by R. H. Cole, B.D. ,"Anglican Church," p. 16.

as the most Western nation[1]; but surely after the conquest, the Britons, a true branch of the Celts, would be known to a Roman as the most Western nation subject to Rome. Many expressions of the early Fathers warrant this interpretation of the words used by Clement.

Theodoret (A.D. 450), having before mentioned the tradition of some of the Apostles having preached in Britain, goes on to say that St. Paul, after his release from imprisonment at Rome, proceeded to Spain and to the "*Islands that lie in the ocean*, and brought salvation to them."[2]   In another passage he says, "Our fishermen and publicans, and *he who was a tentmaker*, carried the evangelical precepts to all nations; not only to those who lived under the Roman jurisdiction, but also to the Scythians and the Hunns; besides to the Indians, the *Britains*, and Germans."[3]   We have, therefore, no hesitation in agreeing with the learned Camden, when he says, "From these authorities it follows, not only that the Gospel was preached in Britain in the times of the Apostles, but that St. Paul himself was the preacher of it."   "Of St. Paul's journey to Britain," writes Bishop Burgess, "we have as satisfactory proof as any historical question can demand."

Gildas, the Wise, a native historian, and the first historian of the British Church, and Abbot of Bangor,

---

[1] Cole, p. 16.

[2] ταῖς ἐν τῷ πελάγει διακειμέναις νήσοις.   *Theodoret* in Psalm cxvi. and in 2 Timothy iv. 17.   *Vide* also authorities cited by Bishop Wordsworth, New Testament with Notes, Introduction to Epistles to Timothy and Titus, Eng. Ed., p. 429.

[3] Theod. Serm. IX. de legibus, Tom. IV., p. 610.   Paris, 1642.   *Vide* Kip's *Double Witness*, p. 124.

wrote about A.D. 560. After giving an account of the victory gained by Suetonius Paulinus over Queen Boadicea, and of the terrible cruelty and sufferings that accompanied it, he goes on to say, " *In the meantime*" (*i.e.*, the time of which he had spoken, viz., the revolt and overthrow of Queen Boadicea, A.D. 61) " Christ, the true Sun, cast its rays, that is, the knowledge of His laws, on this island, shivering with icy cold, and widely separated from the visible sun ; that is to say, not from the visible firmament, but from the supreme, everlasting power of heaven." [1]   These words of our historian, "*in the meantime*," in the opinion of many, fix the date of the introduction of Christianity at this very time.   It is more probable, however, that he refers to a rekindling or reviving of a flame already kindled.   Hore says,[2] " Gildas appears to speak of a double shining of the Gospel, one at the end of the reign of Tiberius, the other, A.D. 61, confined to Britain."

Now as the defeat of Boadicea took place in the year 61, and the martyrdom of St. Paul did not occur till about 68, it is not at all improbable that he entered Britain and preached the Gospel there, between the year 58, when he was released from imprisonment, and 61, when Boadicea was defeated by the Romans.

---

[1] Gildas' Hist. 6.   Hore's *Eighteen Centuries*, etc., p. 15.

[2] *Eighteen Centuries*, etc., p. 15, note.   *Vide* also " supra," notes.
The whole passage reads : " Interea glaciali frigore rigenti insulæ, et velut longiore terrarum secessu soli visibili non proximæ verus ille Sol, non de firmamento solum temporali, sed de summâ etiam cœlorum arce cuncta tempora excedente, orbi universo præfulgidum sui coruscum ostentans, tempore ut scimus, summo Tiberii Cæsaris, quo absque ullo impedimento ejus propagabatur religio, comminata, senatu nolente, a principe morte dilatoribus militum ejusdem, radios suos primum indulget, id est sua præcepta Christus." Hore calls this sentence " flowery and obscure." Id., p. 15.

To these authorities of the first six centuries may be added the later, but very high testimony of *Archbishop Parker*,[1] who states his persuasion that St. Paul preached the Gospel to the Britons, in the interval between his first and second imprisonment at Rome. We further learn, from *Archbishop Usher*, who cites many authorities for his assertion, that St. Paul did not leave the island before he had appointed the first bishop or bishops, and the other ministers of the Church—that Aristobulus was the Bishop he first appointed—and that the three orders of Bishop, Priest, and Deacon, were arranged by St. Paul for the future government of the Church.[2]

Against this vast array of ancient writers may be set the investigations of several modern authors, and when we have allowed to their investigations all the credit to which they are entitled, we shall be forced to the conclusion that there is a very strong presumption, in the weight of evidence, in favour of St. Paul's having visited Britain.   The conclusion is surely justified.

The unvarying tradition of antiquity points out St. Paul as the Apostle by whom the doctrines of the Cross were preached on that island.   That he had *time and opportunity* to visit Britain, has been clearly shown by Bishop Stillingfleet, as well as by the other authors already quoted.   Indeed if he did not go, then there is a *hiatus*, extending over several years of his life, of which we have no account whatever.   Part, certainly, and probably the greater part, of this period was spent in Britain, in Siluria or Cambria, beyond the bounds of

---

[1] *De Vetust. Eccl. Brit.*   Vide *Perranzabuloe*, Trelawny, p. 36.

[2] Usher, *Brit. Eccles. Antiq.*, p. 5.   *Vide* Trelawny, p. 37.

the Roman empire ; and hence the comparative silence of the Greek and Latin writers upon it. That he had *inducements* to go there can be no manner of doubt. Everything invited him to Britain to join the missionary (Aristobulus) whom he had already commissioned to spread the Gospel there, and to be the guest of the royal parent of Claudia. Considering the combination of circumstances which now favoured the execution of his long cherished desire to visit Western Europe, we should regard it as almost extraordinary if he had not gone thither.

As we have already seen, there were Britons, not a few, whose acquaintance St. Paul had made at Rome, who would earnestly desire him to visit their island. One of these was *Linus*, a particular friend of St. Paul, mentioned by him in his Second Epistle to Timothy (iv. 21), and ordained, most likely, by SS. Paul and Peter as first Bishop of Rome. He was, as we have already seen, a native of Britain, and son of Caractacus.[1]

[1] It may be asked, Is there any direct contemporary evidence that *Linus*, the first Bishop of Rome, was the son of Caractacus, and brother of Claudia of Britain? We reply, Yes; apart altogether from British genealogies and tradition, we have a contemporary of St. Paul and of Linus, a resident of Rome, asserting the fact. *Clemens Romanus*, who is mentioned by St. Paul, states in his Epistle—the genuineness of which has never been questioned—that Linus was brother of Claudia. "*Sanctissimus Linus, frater Claudiæ.*" In the Oxford Ed. of Junius, published A.D. 1633, by an error, we find "Son of Claudia." St. Paul lived, according to all evidence, when he was in Rome, whether in custody at large (*libera custodia*) or free, in the bosom of the Claudian family. There is no dispute that Claudia herself was purely British, and the British character of the family, as well as the close domestic ties of affection, between this family and St. Paul, are manifest. If a doubt remained as to whether Linus, first Bishop of Rome, was brother of the Claudia mentioned by St. Paul, the evidence of Irenæus is conclusive as to their identity. He writes, A.D. 180, "The Apostles having founded and built up the Church at Rome, committed its supervision to Linus. This is the Linus mentioned by St. Paul in his Epistle to Timothy." Irenaci *Opera*, Lib. iii., c. 1.

Another was *Claudia Rufina*, the wife of Rufus Pudens, celebrated by the poet Martial,[1] and mentioned by St. Paul in his second Epistle to Timothy.

Yet another was *Pomponia Græcina* (Gladys, sister of Caractacus), wife of Aulus Plautius, the lieutenant of Claudius at the time of Boadicea's defeat. This lady, according to Tacitus,[2] "was accused of embracing the rites of a *foreign superstition*, and ever after led her life in deep sadness and continual melancholy." "For forty years she made use of no habit but what was sorrowful, and expressed no sentiment but what was mournful." "Nothing could alleviate her affliction." These being the well-known characteristics of a primitive Christian, as a pagan would express them, there can be no doubt but the "foreign superstition" was Christianity. And as Pomponia took extraordinary pains to introduce the Roman literature among her countrymen, we may be sure that one so seriously impressed would be equally anxious to have the Gospel preached to them, and that she would do all in her power to induce St. Paul to undertake a mission to her country after his mission to Spain.[3]

[1] "Claudia, Rufe, meo nubit peregrina Pudenti." Vide *Perranzabuloe*, Trelawny, p. 39. Also the *Anglican Church*, Cole, pp. 24-37, where the subject is considered at length.

[2] *Annal.*, lib. xiii., c. 32.

[3] Though some may argue that the traditions of Joseph of Arimathæa, of Linus and Claudia, and of St. Paul, do not rank as authentic history, yet, as has been shown, there are sufficient corroborative circumstances to make historians treat the legends (if such they are) with respect, and to point to the conclusion that by whatever missionaries the Gospel was brought, it reached Britain in the earliest ages. As the epoch of tradition expands into history, we find the British Church covering the land. The details may be uncertain, but the general facts of the case are not to be disputed. Indeed, the most certain truths of the Bible have been surrounded by legends and falsehoods ; the

Besides all this, we find in the ancient British language certain triads which have ever been known as the "*Triads of St. Paul the Apostle.*" They are not found *totidem verbis,* either whole or fragmentarily, in his Epistles, but the morality which they inculcate is quite in keeping with his preaching and his Epistles. We give a few of these triads below, extracted from Morgan's "*St. Paul in Britain.*"

TRIADS.

"There are three sorts of men : The man of God, who renders good for evil; the man of men, who renders good for good and evil for evil ; and the man of the devil, who renders evil for good."

"Three kinds of men are the delight of God : The meek ; the lovers of peace ; the lovers of mercy."

"There are three marks of the children of God : Gentle deportment ; a pure conscience ; patient suffering of injuries."

"There are three ways a Christian punishes an enemy : By forgiving him ; by not divulging his wickedness ; by doing him all the good in his power."

"Three persons have the claims of brothers and sisters : The widow ; the orphan ; the stranger."

The evangelical simplicity of these precepts, contrasting so forcibly with monkish and mediæval inven-

records of history have been corrupted. In each case our duty is to separate the true from the false, and not to reject the true because of the false.

Therefore, when *all* the disciples, except the Apostles, were "scattered abroad," after the persecution which arose about Stephen, and went "*every-where* preaching the Word," it is but natural that some of them should go to Britain, the land of the Druids, where the Roman Governors could not persecute, and where the Druids would extend to them religious toleration.

tions and superstitions, favours their traditional claim to Pauline origin.

The foundation of the great Abbey at Bangor Iscoed is assigned by tradition to St. Paul. Its discipline and doctrine were known "as the rule of Paul" (Pauli Regula), and over each of the four gates was engraved his precept, "If a man will not work, neither let him eat." Its abbots regarded themselves as his successors; they were always men of the highest grade in society, and often of royal blood. Bede and other writers state the number of monks in it to have been 2,100. The scholars amounted to many thousands. Pelagius was its twentieth abbot. St. Hilary and St. Benedict term it, "*Mater omnium monasteriorum*"—the mother of all monasteries.

Of St. Paul's life after he left Britain few particulars have come down to us. After visiting Asia we find him, in the last scene of his life, returned to the bosom of the British royal family at Rome. In his farewell charge to Timothy he sends him the greetings of " Pudens and Linus and Claudia." These, with that of Eubulus, the cousin of Claudia, are the only names of the Christian band mentioned by him; these ministered to him on the eve of his martyrdom, and these attended him when he was on the block of the state lictor, a little distance out of Rome,[1] and these consigned his remains with their own hands to the Pudentinian family tomb on the Ostian Road. Like his Divine Master, "he made his grave with the rich in his death."

[1] *St. Gregory I.*, Bishop of Rome, specifies the " Aquas Salvias," now called " le tre Fontane," on the Via Ostiensis, as the site of his martyrdom. The Chiesa di S. Paola alle tre Fontane preserves the memory of the site.

Linus, Claudia and Pudens, and their four children, when God in His appointed time called them to receive the same crown of the Cross, were buried by his side : the other royal converts, Brân, Caractacus, Cyllinus, and Eurgan died peaceably in Britain, and were interred in the Cor of Ilid in Siluria. All—kings, heroes, apostles, martyrs, saints—were united in the kingdom of light, in the joy of their Lord.[1]

---

[1] The four children of Pudens and Claudia, Timotheus, Novatus, Praxedes and Pudentiana, with their father Pudens, sealed at different times their faith with their blood in Rome, and were, with Linus, the first Britons who were added to the glorious army of martyrs. And, Pudens excepted, they were not only martyrs, but royal martyrs ; and martyrs of the most patriotic and heroic blood in Britain.

Linus suffered A.D. 90 ; Pudens, 96 ; Pudentiana, in the Third Persecution, 107 ; Novatus, in the Fifth Persecution, 139, when his brother Timotheus is believed to have been absent in Britain, baptizing his nephew, King Lucius. Soon after his return from Britain, and in extreme old age, about his ninetieth year, Timotheus suffered, with his fellow-soldier Marcus, in the same city of Rome, "drunk with the blood of the martyrs of Jesus." Praxedes, the surviving sister, received her crown during the same year. Claudia alone died a natural death (in Samnium) before any of her children, A.D. 97, surviving her husband one year. They were all interred by the side of St. Paul on the side of the Via Ostiensis. Vide *St. Paul in Britain*, Morgan, pp. 196, 197.

Pudens, we have seen, died A.D. 96. About this time St. John wrote his Second Epistle, in which he " exhorteth a certain honourable matron, with her children, to persevere in Christian love and faith." May not this Epistle have been addressed to *Claudia* by St. John? These words would help to console her in her affliction. It applies to her exactly. Claudia followed Pudens to eternal life, as was said above, in A.D. 97. All these died in faith.

CHAPTER II.

THE CHURCH IN BRITAIN FROM THE CLOSE OF THE FIRST CENTURY TO THE ESTABLISHMENT OF THE HEPTARCHY.

LUCIUS—PERSECUTION—COUNCILS—TESTIMONY OF EARLY WRITERS—PELAGIAN HERESY—INSTITUTIONS OF LEARNING—PARISH CHURCHES, ORIGIN OF—"ALLELUIA VICTORY"—THE SAXON INVASION—THE SAXON HEPTARCHY—BRITISH CHRISTIANS DRIVEN INTO WALES—EMINENT MEN: DUBRICIUS, ST. DAVID, SAMPSON, ST. CADOC, ST. PADARN, ST. TEILO, ST. ILLTYD, ST. KENTIGERN, ST. ASAPH, ST. DANIEL (OR DEINIOL), GILDAS THE HISTORIAN—THE MONKS, KINDNESS TO ANIMALS—THE MONKS, OUR INDEBTEDNESS TO—WALES, EARLY HISTORY OF, WRITTEN ON ITS SURFACE—HYMN TO THE CHURCH IN WALES.

IT could scarcely be expected that a people so savage as the Britons, so devoted to their superstitions, and so depressed by their fierce invaders, could speedily be converted to the Christian Faith. The branch of the spiritual vine, therefore, though planted so early in the soil of Britain, was, from the nature of things, slow in its growth, and during the first century did not make rapid progress. By the middle of the second century, however, " She had sent out her boughs unto the sea, and her branches unto the river " ; for it is evident that, by that time, a large number of the inhabitants, of all ranks, had abandoned idolatry and had embraced the Christian Faith.

We have already seen [1] that the *first Church* ever built in Britain, and probably in Christendom, was erected at Glastonbury in the first century. The old Saxon historians agree that St. Peter's Church, Cornhill, London, was founded about A.D. 179, and that it was afterwards the Cathedral Church of the Archbishop of London. Theanus, who died *circ.* A.D. 187, is thought to have been its founder and first Archbishop.

The following item appeared in the " Liverpool Times " for Sep. 26th, 1879 :

" The Church of St. Peter-upon-Cornhill, London, has recently celebrated its traditionary seventeenth centennial. It is said to have been founded by the first missionaries to Britain, 179 A.D."

The late Archbishop of Canterbury (Dr. Tait) preached in St. Peter's, on the occasion of the commemoration referred to above, and in his sermon referred, in eloquent terms, to the ancient tradition concerning this Church, and also to the introduction of Christianity into Britain at an early period of the Christian Era.

Before the Great Fire of London a brass plate was kept in St. Peter-upon-Cornhill and another in St. Paul's Cathedral, on which the following inscription was engraved in the old style of spelling : [2]

" Be it known to all Men that in the Yeerys of our Lord God An. CLXXIX., Lucius, the fyrst Christen Kyng of this Land, then callyd Brytayne, foundyd the fyrst Chyrch in London, that is to sey, the Chyrch of Sent Peter, APON Cornhyl ; and he foundyd there an Arch-

---

[1] Page 37.

[2] A facsimile of the old brass tablet may still be seen in the sacristy of St. Peter's, and from it this inscription was copied.

byshop's See and made that Chyrch the Metropolitant and cheef Chyrch of this Kyngdom ; and so enduryd the space of CCCC yeerys and more, unto the commyng of Sent Austin, an Apostyl of Englend, the whych was sent into the Land by Sent Gregory, the Doctor of the Chyrch in the tyme of Kyng Ethelbert, and then was the Archbyshop's See and Pol removyd from the afore-sayed Chyrch of St. Peter APON Cornhyl unto Dere-bernaum, that now is callyd Canterbury, and there yt remeynyth to this Day."

LUCIUS.[1]

An event of the highest importance contributed greatly, at this period, to forward the progress of the Christian Faith. We find (A.D. 167)[2] a British ruler not only professing the Christian religion himself, but becoming "a nursing father" to the infant Church. This illustrious prince was *Lucius*, who, in his zeal for the conversion of all his subjects, sent two of his learned men (Elvanus and Medvinus) to Rome for the purpose of consulting Elutherius, then Bishop of Rome, as to the best measures to adopt for that purpose. The Bishop received the messengers gladly, instructed them more perfectly in the Christian religion, and sent them back to Lucius (together with two of his own trusted messengers) with a present of "bothe the Oulde and Newe Testaments,"[3] and also a letter containing these

---

[1] Lewer Mawr, in Latin, Lucius.

[2] Bede says 156 A.D. According to Usher the date is fixed by some as early as 137. These earlier dates are open to objection.

[3] Sir W. Dethicke—Vide *Collect. of Curious Disc.* Vol. II., p. 165.

remarkable words: " You have received in the kingdom of Britain, by God's mercy, both the law and faith of Christ. You have both the Old and New Testament. Out of the same, through God's grace, by the advice of your realme, take a law, and by the same, through God's sufferance, *rule you your kingdom of Britain, for in that kingdom you are God's vicar.*" [1]

In this remarkable as well as valuable document we have four things distinctly admitted by a Bishop of Rome, viz.—the existence and nationality of the British Church—her right to administer her own affairs—her independence of the See of Rome—and the supremacy of the ruler of Britain (over all persons and causes) within his own dominions. This is surely a most important admission, and when coupled with the fact that Christianity was thus publicly professed in Britain by the ruling power, 146 years before it was so acknowledged at Rome,[2] it places at an immeasurable distance the Pope's pretended right to supreme authority over the Church and kingdom of Britain.

And Lucius was a man worthy of a crown. In the full spirit of independence he commenced his holy undertaking. He converted (A.D. 168) three Pagan Arch-Flamins and twenty-eight Flamins into so many Archbishops and Bishops,[3] and appointed the Arch-

---

[1] Prideaux's *Introduc. to Hist.* Quoted in Trelawny's *Perranzabuloe*, pp. 55-57. *Vide* also Foot-note, p. 7.

[2] Constantine did not proclaim Christianity as the religion of the State at Rome till A.D. 313.

[3] Mr. Agarde, A.D. 1604, quotes from "a large booke of St. Augustine's of Canterbury," written about the year 1406, as follows :—" Lucius, primus rex Christianus regni istius, sub anno Dom. 167, qui fuit annus 430 ante adventum

bishops to London, York, and Caerleon in Wales. The idol temples were destroyed, churches were erected in several parts of the island,[1] and various privileges and estates were granted for their support and honour.[2]

Such, then, is part of the historical evidence of the early establishment of Christianity in Britain, and no one can deny that among such a mass of testimony there must be some truth. Nor can we dispose of the traditions and statements, already given, by supposing them to be the creation of diseased brains of monks of the middle ages. There are too many concurrent probabilities to allow of this; too many well-known facts and events harmonized; too much presumptive, circumstantial, and indirect evidence to warrant such a supposition. And in every succeeding age we can clearly trace the onward progress of the cause. The Venerable Bede tells us of kings who gloried in the Cross of Christ and sought to aid its triumphs, and to this cause we must ascribe the gradual dying out of the superstitions of the Druids, which, after the second century of Christianity, are no longer met with in the history of the country.

On the death of Lucius, A.D. 208, Severus, a Roman, succeeded to the crown of Britain, and there is abundant evidence that, through the patronage of princes, and especially of Coill, whose daughter *Helena* married Con-

Augustini. Qui Lucius divisit regnum in tres Archiepiscopatus, scilicit, Londinum Eboracum et Civitatem Legionensium, id est, Westcestre." *Collect. of Curious Disc.*, Vol. II., p. 160.

For further information concerning Lucius, *vide* Cole's *Anglican Church*, pp. 42-44.

[1] St. Martin's at Canterbury being probably one of them.

[2] Prideaux's *Introduc. to Hist.*

stantius Chlorus, the father of Constantine, Christianity made such rapid progress in the island as to call forth the observation from Origen, that "the divine goodness of God our Saviour *is equally* diffused amongst the Britons, the Africans, and the other nations of the world."[1]

PERSECUTION.

Nor did her remote situation shield her from the rage of persecution. That which was commenced under Diocletian (A.D. 303), on as vain a pretext as that of *Nero* (viz., the burning of his palace at Nicomedia), exceeded in severity all that had gone before it, and was, unfortunately, a check to the growing prosperity of the Church. Its fury was directed against Christian temples, the Bible, and persons of every age, sex, and rank. Its rage was felt in every part of the Roman Empire. It extended into Britain, where the numbers who were cruelly tortured and put to death afford no insignificant proof of the progress that Christianity had made there by that time. But here, as elsewhere, "the blood of the martyrs was the seed of the Church." Foremost in that glorious band who "counted not their lives dear unto themselves," the annals of the day tell us of *St. Alban*, of Verulam, whose name till this day remains in the scene of his simple faith, when more than fifteen hundred years have passed away. This proto-martyr of the British Church suffered on the 17th day of Juue, A.D. 305, and his name is retained in the calendar of the Church of England. We might also

[1] Orig. Hom. VI.

mention the distinguished names of Julius, Bishop of Caerleon ; Aaron, Bishop of Exeter ; and Angulius, Bishop of London ; all of whom suffered martyrdom during these fiery times.

This persecution was crushed out, in Britain, after two years' duration, by the authority of Constantius Chlorus [1] (the ruler of Britain at that time), on his own authority, and even at the risk of a civil war. Then the Christians came forth from the caves and forests where they had been concealed, rebuilt their churches, and renewed the rites of Christian worship unmolested ; [2] and under the special protection of Constantine, his son and successor, [3] Christianity flourished beyond all former times, and many additional churches were erected.

COUNCILS.

The importance to which the Church had arrived, at the early part of the fourth century, is demonstrated by the fact that British Bishops were present and assisted at the early Councils of the Church. In A.D. 314, the Council of *Arles* was convened by Constantine, from all parts of the West, to take action in regard to the *Donatist* controversy. At that time York, London, and Caerleon were the capitals of the three Roman provinces of Britain, viz., Maxima Cæsariensis, Britannia Prima, and Britannia Secunda. And it is interesting to note that the Church of Britain was represented by three Bishops (attended by a priest and a deacon), who

[1] Constantius married the British Princess *Helena*, who, most assuredly, was a Christian.   [2] Camden's *Brit.*

[3] Constantine was born at York. His mother was a lineal descendant of Caractacus, and he became the *first* Christian Emperor of Rome.

came from the three capitals above referred to, and that they were recognized by the two hundred Bishops there assembled, as representatives of a true branch of the Church, possessing the Catholic Creed and an Apostolic ministry. In the Corbury MS., which Haddon and Stubbs adjudge to be the best authority, the names stand in the following order :—

"Eborius Episcopus de civitate Eboracensi provincia Britannia.

Restitutus Episcopus de civitate Londinensi provincia suprascripta.

Adelfius Episcopus de civitate Colonia Londinensium.

Exinde Sacerdos presbyter ; Arminius diaconus."

The *first* and *second* are designated as the Bishops of York and of London respectively. The *third, Adelfius,* is designated as Bishop of "*Colonia Londinensium.*" This has created some confusion among scholars. It is unquestionably an error of the transcriber, the most probable emendation being the substitution (for " Londinensium ") of *Legionensium* — Caerleon-upon-Usk. "*Colonia*" being the equivalent for "*Caer.*"[1]

Again, in the year 325, British Bishops were (almost certainly) present at the Council of *Nice,* summoned by Constantine to decide the heresy of Arius. There is no *express* evidence that British Bishops were present, for the subscriptions are confused and imperfect. The language of St. Athanasius,[2] however, would indicate their personal presence, and the connection of Constantine with Britain would, *à priori,* lead us to expect that

---

[1] *Vide* Stillingfleet, *Antiq,* ii. ; *Opp.* Vol. III., 48. Haddon and Stubbs, *Concilia,* 7.

[2] *Vide* Pryce, *Anct. Bt. Ch.* Note, p. 95.

his comprehensive and pressing invitation would be accepted and acted upon. Eusebius says he summoned Bishops out of all provinces,[1] and provided them with carriages, and other accommodation for their journey ; and that the most eminent Bishops of all Churches, as well those of Europe as of Asia, did come to Nice. Eusebius, as we have already seen, was well acquainted with the Church of Britain ; and it is not probable that Constantine, who had summoned British Bishops to the less important Council of Arles, would neglect to summon them to the much more important one of Nice. The result of this great Council was the condemnation of Arius ; the Nicene Creed, as far as the words " I believe in the Holy Ghost " ; the decision as to the proper time for keeping Easter ; and the adoption of twenty Canons.

British Bishops, it is asserted, were also present at the Council of *Sardica*, in A.D. 347 ; and there is convincing evidence that they attended the Synod of *Ariminium*, too, in A.D. 359, where Bishops from all parts of the West had assembled. It would seem that a considerable number of them attended this latter Council, from the statement that, although the Aquitanians, Gauls, and Britons generally declined the hospitality of the Emperor, three of the British Bishops were induced, from poverty, to accept it, rather than burden private individuals.[2]

---

[1] ἀπανταχοθεν τοὺς ἐπισκόπους γράμμασι τιμητικοῖς.

[2] Sulpicius Severus, writing about A.D. 400, says : "this" (viz., to use the Emperor's hospitality) " seemed unseemly to our Bishops, and to the Gauls and Britons . . . Three only from Britain, through poverty, availed themselves of the public provision." Haddon and Stubbs, *Concilia*, i., p. 10.

It is a noteworthy fact, connected with the former of these Councils, which, as bearing on the supremacy of Rome, should not be lost sight of, that the decrees of of that Council were sent by the British Bishops to the Bishop of Rome, to be *promulgated*, and not, as Romanists pretend, to be confirmed. In their letter to the Bishop, they give him none of those pompous titles which the Popes of Rome have since assumed; but they call him their "dear brother." They say that they were knit together in one common bond of charity and unity—that they were met at Arles, *in obedience to their most pious Emperor*—that they would have been glad of *the company of their brother, the Bishop of Rome*, but as that could not be, they had sent him an abstract of their canons, that he *might publish it throughout his diocese*.[1] Such were the sentiments expressed by this important Council—sentiments worthy of the purity and independence of the British Church. They show that no such thing as the arrogant claims of the Bishop of Rome, to control over her, was known at that time.

TESTIMONY OF EARLY WRITERS.

From this time forward, Fathers of the Church and other writers furnish abundant testimony to the existence, purity and continuity of the Faith in the British Isles. A few of these testimonies will be interesting.

I. *Justin Martyr*, born about A.D. 103, one of the earliest and most learned of the Christian Fathers, wrote about a century after the Ascension of our Lord.

---

[1] Guthrie's *Hist. of Eng.*, Vol. I., p. 75. See also *Perranzabuloe*, Trelawny, pp. 59, 60.

He states that there were Christians in every country known to the Romans.

2. *Irenæus*, a pupil of the eminent Polycarp of Smyrna, was consecrated Bishop of Lyons, in Gaul, A.D. 177. He says that the Church was extended by the Apostles to the utmost bounds of the earth. If, in this statement, he included the Celts of Gaul, he would also include the Celts of Britain.

3. *Tertullian*, born in Carthage A.D. 160, was the first of the Latin writers of the Church. He says (about A.D. 190), that Christianity in Britain, had penetrated even to those parts inaccessible to the Roman arms.[1] Now the Romans, when he wrote, had extended as far as to the wall of Hadrian. It follows, therefore, that he means that Christianity had extended beyond this wall, even to the Picts who were not conquered by Rome. The Hadrian wall extended right across the north of Britain from Carlisle to Tynemouth, and Christianity had penetrated still farther north, even at this early period.

4. *Origen*, who wrote about twenty or thirty years later, confirms the statement of Tertullian. He says, "The power of God our Saviour is even with them in Britain, who are separated from our world."[2] Yet we learn from the same author that some parts of the Islands had not yet heard of the Gospel.[3]

---

[1] Et Britannorum inaccessa Romanis loca, Christo vera subdita. "Quando enim terra Britanniæ ante adventum Christi in unius Dei consensit Religionem." —H. in Ezech. IV. See *The Anglican Church*, Cole, p. 47.

[2] "Virtus Domini Salvatoris et cum his est qui ab orbe in Britannia dividuntur, et cum his qui in Maritania," . . . etc.—Hom. IV., Inter. Hier.

[3] "Plurimi nondum audiverunt Evangelii verbum." St. Matt. Com. V.. 39.

5. *The Diocletian Persecution* (A.D. 303-5), as we have already seen, reached Britain, and during its continuance many British Christians yielded their lives a willing sacrifice to the cause of Christ. The Emperor commanded the Governor to burn all Christian books, and to destroy their places of worship. Christians who refused to deny their Lord were to be tortured and put to death.[1] Amongst those who suffered death were St. Alban of Verulam, Julius of Caerleon, Aaron of Exeter, and Angulius of London.[2]

6. *Eusebius* expressly says (A.D. 320) that some of the Apostles "passed over the ocean to those which are called the British islands."

7. *St. Athanasius* (A.D. 350) testifies to the fidelity of the Britons to the purity of the Faith, as settled at Nicæa,[3] and ranks the British Bishops with the prelates of various provinces, who adhered to the decision of the Sardican Council, against those who had libelled his character by the way of striking at the Faith which he upheld."[4]

8. *St. Chrysostom* (about A.D. 400) says that "the British islands, situated beyond our sea, and lying in the very ocean, have felt the power of the Word, for even there churches are built and altars erected."[5] In

---

[1] Gildas' *Hist.* VII. *Vide* also " Drych y Prifoesoedd," Pt. II., p. 159. Sulp. Sever. Hist. Sac. I. 4, p. 302.

[2] See above, pp. 41, 42.

[3] " This Faith all the fathers assembled at Nicæa confessed ; and all the Churches in every place concurred with it ; those of Spain, Britain and Gaul." *Epist. ad Jovian Imp.*

[4] Bright, *Early Eng. Ch.*, Chap. I., p. 12.

[5] καὶ γὰρ κἀκεῖ ἐκκλησίας καὶ θυσιαστήρια πεπέγασιν.—Chrys. Quod. Chr. Sid. Deus, 12.

another place he says of the Britons : " Their language is an awkward and imperfect one, but in their principles, respecting religion, they harmonize delightfully ; they are correct. Their language, it is true, is absurd, rough, and coarse, but their morals are meek and holy "—to which adds the author of " Drych y Prifoesoedd ": " He thought their language was rough and clumsy because he did not understand it." [1]

9. *St. Hilary*, of Poitiers, being banished into Phrygia by Constantius, writing from his exile (about A.D. 358) sends greeting to the British, in common with all other Christian Bishops. He laments that his banishment prevented him from hearing from them as he had been accustomed ; but though he had this inconvenience, he had the highest satisfaction in learning that the British were remarkable for their strict adherence to the genuine doctrines of Christianity, and he congratulates them " that they have remained undefiled in the Lord and unhurt by all contagion of heresy " [2] (the Arian).

10. *St. Jerome* testifies to the passion and resurrection of Christ being " known from India to Britain," [3] and in another place says that Britain " worships the same Christ, observes the same rule of faith as other nations."

11. And to quote from another author, the *Venerable*

---

[1] " Drych y Pryfoes.," Pt. II., Cap. IV., pp. 166, 167.

[2] " Dilectissimis et beatissimis partibus et Coepiscopis . . . et provinciarum Britanniarum episcopis," . . . etc. *De Synodis.* See also Haddon and Stubbs, I., p. 9 ; Hore's *Eighteen Cent. of the Ch. in Eng.*, II., p. 32 ; Bright, *Early Eng. Ch.*, Cap. I., pp. 12, 13 ; Newell, *An. Bt. Ch.*, Cap. III., p. 22 ; Cole, *The Anglican Ch.*, p. 50.

[3] Ep. XXXV., ad Hel. Ep. 146, 1. Quoted by Bright.

Bede tells us[1] that from the time of the British King Lucius, "the Britons preserved the Faith they had received, uncorrupted and entire, in peace and tranquility, until the time of the Emperor Diocletian," who disturbed them in the fourth century with a cruel persecution.[2]

In the third year of Theodosius the Great (A.D. 381), at the Council assembled at Constantinople, by order of that Emperor—and not by the Bishop of Rome, as asserted by Baronius—principally for the purpose of defining the limits of Bishoprics, it was ordered that the several provincial Bishops should have their ancient privileges of independence confirmed to them ; and this confirmation was grounded on the *Sixth Canon* of the Council of Nicæa. In that Canon it is enjoined, that " in the provinces *everywhere,* none of the most religious Bishops shall invade another province, which has not been for many years before, and from the beginning, under *his,* or his predecessor's hand." Now in applying the acts of this Council to the state of the British Church, at the time of which we are speaking, we are assisted by a very ancient Greek MS. in the Bodleian Library, purporting to be " the Order of the Presidency of the Most Holy Patriarchs " on this occasion, wherein neither England, Scotland, nor Ireland, are reckoned dependents upon the Roman Patriarchate. So that we have evidence most satisfactory and convincing of the inde-

[1] Book I., Chap. IV.

[2] Alban, the proto-martyr of Britain, was slain during this persecution, A.D. 305. When the storm was over, the Christians rebuilt their churches. Bede, Lib. I., c. 8.

pendence of the British Church down to the close of the fourth century.

PELAGIAN HERESY.

The history of the Church is involved in some obscurity, between the death of Constantine and the final abandonment of Britain by the Romans in A.D. 448. It is distinctly known, however, that during this period, the Church was outwardly afflicted by the sanguinary incursions of the *Picts and Scots*, and inwardly it was harassed by the Pelagian heresy which, according to both Bede and Gildas, dates from this time.   This heresy was introduced into Britain by Agricola, son of a Gallican Bishop (Severianus).   The author of it was Pelagius, a Briton by birth, and usually called Morgan. He, during a residence at Rome, by associating with Rufinus, a man deeply imbued with the principles of Origen, began to deny the doctrine of original sin.   The heresy soon spread through the island.   The leading Bishops, who were generally sound in the Faith, for some time resisted the pernicious doctrine ; but becoming alarmed at the spread of Pelagianism, and despairing of their own efforts to put it down, they sent for help to the Bishops of the neighbouring Church of Brittany in Gaul.   The Gallican Bishops summoned a Council at Troyes, and sent over, in answer to the appeal (probably in A.D. 429) *St. German*, Bishop of Auxerre, a Breton by birth, and *Lupus*,[1] Bishop of Troyes, men of great reputation.   They, by public preaching in the

---

[1] Some of the oldest Parish Churches in Wales bear the name of German and Lupus (the latter in its Welsh form, *Bleiddian*), to this day.

fields and streets, and by arguments advanced before a public conference at Verulam succeeded in suppressing the heresy for a time; and the triumph of orthodoxy appearing complete, the Bishops returned to Gaul, leaving the Britons, as they supposed, established in the faith, and the Pelagians convinced of their error.

But the heresy broke out afresh, and *St. German* was induced again to visit Britain (A.D. 447) taking with him this time *Severus,* Bishop of Troyes, a disciple of Lupus, his former colleague. Their labours were successful. Pelagianism was again extirpated, and the heretical teachers were banished. Bede says, that " from that time forward the British Church continued sound and orthodox." Means were now taken, to effectually perpetuate this great triumph, which proved a priceless blessing to the Church and to the country.

INSTITUTIONS OF LEARNING FOUNDED.

Schools or Monasteries were established in different parts of Wales. One of these was at *Llandaff* under *Dubricius;* another at Llanilltyd Fawr, now called *Llantwit Major,* in Glamorganshire, under *Illtyd* or Illutus, where many of the English nobility were educated. The famous Monastery of *Bangor-Iscoed* was also founded at the same time, if not through the exertions of St. German, certainly on his advice and recommendation. All these schools became celebrated. It is said that the one under *Dubricius* at Llandaff, had not less than a thousand pupils. Great numbers flocked to it from all parts of Britain, and among its pupils were *SS. Teilo* and *Sampson.* Scarcely less

famous, and to a dweller in Glamorganshire more interesting, was the College of *Illtyd* or Illutus, one of his
pupils being the renowned *Gildas*.   Another famous seat
of learning was the Monastery of *Llancarvan*, in Glamorganshire, founded by *St. Cadoc*, and of which he
became the first abbot.   To this institution were admitted, not only candidates for the monastic life, but also
the sons of the chiefs and petty kings of Wales ; so that
it became celebrated both for religious and secular
learning.   It was followed by many other places of
learning usually bearing the name of Bangor, *i.e.*, " high
choir, or circle."   We referred a moment ago to Bangor-
Iscoed ("under the wood ").   It is said to have contained
two thousand monks at the time of its destruction
by King Ethelred, twelve hundred of whom were
massacred.[1]   Another *Bangor* was that which still bears
the name, and of which David was (as was not uncom-
mon) both Abbot and Bishop.   Yet another *Bangor* was
the Monastery of *Llanelwy*, now *St. Asaph*, founded under
the direction of Kentigern or St. Mungo, who, with his
pupil St. Asaph, founded that See in the sixth century.
St. Kentigern was also the founder of the See of
Glasgow and its first Bishop.   Into the Monastery of St.
Asaph men of all ranks and ages pressed to the number
of 965.   Besides these, there were the *White House* or
Whitland, founded by Paulinus in Carmarthenshire, at
which *St. David* was educated ; also the great College
of *Llanbadarn Fawr*, founded by *St. Padarn the Great*,
where one of the most remarkable churches in the Prin-
cipality still exists.[2]

[1] Bede, Book II., 2.   [2] Bright's *Early Eng. Ch.*

When we consider that it was the want of learning on the part of the British clergy, which gave a temporary advantage to the followers of Pelagius, and made it necessary for the British clergy to send to Gaul for assistance ; and further, that at that time the Gallican Monasteries were distinguished for their learning and the cultivation of literature, we can easily imagine that St. German would advise the establishment of such schools of learning as those already referred to.   This would account for the origin of the legend which makes him the founder of these institutions.   There are churches, not a few, both in Cornwall and Wales dedicated to St. German.[1]   They are among the earliest, if indeed they are not the earliest, instances in Britain of *Parish Churches.*   Hitherto the work of evangelization appears to have been carried on from certain centres, from which the clergy went forth to preach, and to which they returned to live in community, and to impart by their presence a greater solemnity to the higher offices of religion.   But on the Continent at this time, an organization of a more parochial character was developing.[2]   This circumstance, combined with the new character of the churches of the foundation of St. German, suggests the idea that, at this time, owing to the greater experience and wider knowledge of the Galli-

[1] Llanarmon-in-Iâl, Denbighshire; Llanarmon Dyffryn Ceiriog, ditto; S. Harmon's, Radnorshire ; and the following chapels : Llanarmon under Llangybi, Carnarvonshire : Bettws-Garmon under Llanfair Isgaer, ditto ; Capel Garmon under Llanrwst, Denbighshire ; and Llanarmon-Fach under Llandyfan, ditto.   The ancient Cathedral of the Cornish Britons, as well as that in the Isle of Man and Germansweek in Devonshire, were dedicated in his name.

N.B.—The word "*Llan,*" in the old Celtic or British dialect, always means Church.   We find it everywhere in Wales to this day.

[2] Bingham, *Antiq.*, ix. 8, 1. 3.

can Bishops, country churches for permanent use began to be erected, without however, for some centuries, superseding the old central system. Pelagianism seems to have been so completely uprooted by this second mission, and the people so fortified against its future inroads, that it never again revived in Britain.[1]

"THE ALLELUIA VICTORY."

Let us return for a moment to the first mission of St. German to Britain with Lupus. It was at the time that the Picts and Scots had combined to invade the country. About the middle of Lent, A.D. 430, the two missionaries joined the British camp, in which a considerable number of the soldiers were still heathen, and having spent much time in instructing them in the Christian religion, administered to them on Easter Even the Sacrament of Baptism in a rude church constructed of trees and boughs. The place is at Llanarmon, near Mold, on the banks of the Dee. The Britons were surprised by the near approach of a large number of fierce invaders. They advanced at once to repulse them, many of them still wet from the baptismal laver, putting their trust in Divine help, and almost despairing of human power. From these inexperienced troops, German, who had resolved to be their leader himself, selected the most active, and posted his little army in ambush in a narrow valley encompassed by hills.[2] The heathen warriors advanced confident of victory. All of a sudden the priests from the ambush shouted, "Alleluia,

---

[1] Vide *Ancient Brit. Ch.*, Pryce, pp. 123-125.

[2] The place has since been called " Gaes Garmon," or the field of German.

Alleluia, Alleluia," words with which the soldiers had become familiar at their Easter rejoicings. With one voice they took up the shout. The surrounding hills multiplied the echo. It rang from hill to hill, and filled the invading hosts with panic. Thinking that the hills were falling on them, or a mighty multitude pouring out against them, they cast away their arms, and fled in great disorder. Many of them in their mad flight fell into the river, swollen with the spring rains, and were drowned. Thus the great " Alleluia Victory " was gained, the Britons remaining inactive spectators, without striking a single blow or losing a single man.[1]

THE SAXON INVASION.

We have seen that the Church was rescued from the Pelagian heresy but it had more formidable foes to encounter. No longer protected by the powerful countenance of the Roman Emperors, she was now grievously oppressed by the frequent incursions of those predatory tribes who occupied the Northern frontier of Britain— the *Picts* (as the Caledonians were then called), and the *Scots* (a tribe who had migrated from Ireland). In their distress, the people of South Britain sent an appeal to Rome for help, inscribed, " *The Groans of the Britons.*" But there were Northern barbarians at the time threatening Rome itself. The great fabric of the Empire was tottering to its foundation ; and Rome, feeling obliged to concentrate around the capital the scattered forces of of the Empire, had withdrawn her legions from Britain

---

[1] *Vide* Hore's *Eighteen Centuries*, pp. 35, 36.

in A.D. 410. Attila, surnamed " The Scourge of God," with his conquering hordes had crossed the Alps and was advancing on Rome. The Romans had all they could do to defend themselves, and so the petition from Britain was unheeded.

In this extremity of desertion on one hand and suffering on the other, the Britons persuaded *Vortigern*, Prince of Damnonium, to send deputies to the Saxons requesting their assistance. This was an evil hour for the Britons, for of all the German tribes the Saxons were the most warlike and savage. Gildas speaks of "the stupidity and infatuation under which the Britons acted, in calling to their help a nation whom they dreaded more than death." The Saxons readily responded to the request, and under Hengist and Horsa, their leaders, they landed in Britain (A.D. 449), and made short work with the Picts and Scots. This first success speedily brought over more of their adventurous countrymen, who became so charmed with the fertility of the soil, and the mildness of the climate, that they soon assumed the attitude of conquerors; and joining the Picts and Scots against the Britons, by force of arms, they maintained their possession of the country. For a time Britain, unaided and alone, successfully withstood them. Indeed, under Ambrosius Aurelianus, A.D. 489, they seem to have won an important battle at Bannesdown. Ambrosius is said to have employed the respite thus afforded in rebuilding some of the churches which had been destroyed in the war, and in providing for the better settlement of religious affairs. Geoffrey of Monmouth says that he also convened a Council and appointed two metropolitans, Sampson to York and Dubricius to Caerleon. Sampson, we are told, afterwards went to Armorica, and became Archbishop of Dole.[1]

But eventually victory crowned the efforts of the enemy; and never was a victory more complete, or more cruelly misused. Probably of all the hordes that dismembered the Roman Empire, the Saxons were the most barbarous. The Goths and Lombards had been christianized: and the Franks, if not christians, had at least been softened by Roman civilization. But the Saxons were heathen; they worshipped the sun and moon, and Wodin, or Odin, and Thor, the thunderer, and many other false gods.[2] The greatest virtue with them was courage, and the greatest vice was cowardice. And so Britain, from east to west, became involved in rapine and slaughter. Her cruel masters turned their ruthless hands against every thing and person that had a religious character, destroyed every church they could reach, and slew the Christians at the very altars. The Bishops and clergy were hunted down like wild beasts, and they either miserably perished, or else sought refuge in expatriation.

And, as if this condition of things was not already bad enough for the despised and down-trodden Faith, Vortigern, the prince already referred to, married the daughter of Hengist, thus forming a royal alliance with paganism.

The plunder that fell into the hands of these Saxon spoilers attracted the cupidity of other piratical tribes.

---

[1] Collier, Cent. VI.

[2] Yet, strange as it may seem, it is from them that we derive the word "God," or "the Good."

The Jutes and the Angles rushed to the quarry, and with murderous rapidity carried fire and sword to every part of Britain proper. The Britons long maintained the unequal combat, but after a struggle of 150 years, were compelled to receive the yoke of their heartless pagan conquerors.

We can easily understand from the fierce character of the people, how the Teutonic settlement in Britain was quite unlike that of the Goths, the Lombards, or the Franks, in the countries which they conquered. The conquest of Gaul, or of Italy, was little more than a forcible settlement in the conquered country, which was destined in the course of time to absorb the conquerors. French, for instance, is not the language of the Frank, but of the Gaul, whom the Frank conquered. But the German conquest of Britain was a complete dispossession or slaughter of the conquered people. Wherever the conqueror went, the vengeance he took on the Britains was terrible. Whole villages and towns were consigned to the flames, and a promiscuous slaughter of the inhabitants ensued. Everything Celtic was as effectually wiped out of the land as everything Roman was wiped out of Africa by the Saracen conquerors of Carthage.[1] Britain ceased to be Britain, and became England. The religion, the laws, the language were all changed ; and, as if to recall to the people the daily remembrance of their slavery, the very days of the week took the names of the deities which had dethroned Christ.[2]

[1] Freeman's *Norman Conquest.*

[2] Green's *Hist. of the Eng. People.*

Meanwhile, the condition of the British Church was most deplorable. According to Bingham,[1] there must have been in the country, before these calamities came upon it, more Bishops than there are at the present day. By the Anglo-Saxons, the whole of South Britain, which they conquered, and which we know by the name of England, was divided into seven kingdoms, known as the

SAXON HEPTARCHY.

These kingdoms were :—

1. Kent, set up by the		Jutes.
2. Sussex,		
3. Wessex,	}	Saxons.
4. Essex, which included Middlesex		
5. East Anglia,		
6. Northumbria,	}	Angles.
7. Mercia,		

In all these kingdoms Christianity was simply annihilated. Gildas, who wrote about the middle of the sixth century, if not an eye-witness himself, must have conversed with those who had been eye-witnesses of the devastation which he describes. From him we learn that the cities and churches were burned to the ground ; the inhabitants destroyed with the sword, or buried in the ruins of houses and altars, which were defiled with the blood of the slain. He applies to the devastation the words of the Psalmist, " They have cast fire into Thy sanctuary, they have defiled by casting down the dwelling place of Thy name to the ground," and, " O God, the heathen have come into Thine in-

---

[1] *Antiquities of the Christian Ch.*, Book IX., Chap. 6.

heritance : Thy holy temple have they defiled." Bede says that all public and private buildings were destroyed ; the blood of the priests was poured out on the altars ; the prelates and people were destroyed together by fire and sword, and no man dared to give them burial.

But the whole of the western part of the country remained *un*conquered. *Strathclyde,* including the country from the Clyde to the Dee, the Kingdom of Cumbria; *North Wales,* or Cambria ; *South Wales,*[1] and Devon and Cornwall, with part of Somerset and the sacred Avàlon, remained purely British. This land the English called Welsh-land, or the " Land of the Foreigner," Welsh being the name which the Germans applied to all nations speaking languages of Latin descent. For a time, Theon, Bishop of London, and Thadioc, Bishop of York, held to their Sees, at the risk of their lives ; but when the country had entirely lapsed into paganism, when London sacrificed to Diana, and Westminster to Apollo, and they found that all was lost, then, in A.D. 587, they were forced by perse-cution to fly and join their brethren in Wales.

To those parts we must now look *for the Primitive Church of Britain.*   It was shut off from, and perhaps to

---

[1] South Wales was conquered by Henry I. ; North Wales, not till the reign of Edward I. ; while the conquest of Cornwall was effected in the tenth century by King Athelstan. It is said that the chief antagonist of the West Saxons (Wessex) was the renowned *King Arthur*, and that he, at the battle of Mount Badon (Bath), A.D. 520, so stubbornly resisted the Saxon advance, that the territory now known as Cornwall, Devon, and Somerset, then called by the Saxons *West Wales*, was for many years free from further fighting. By this means the famous church of *Glastonbury*, " first ground of the saints," the foundation of Christianity in the land, was preserved from the terrible destruc-tion that fell upon the other churches which the British Christians had built. Lane's *Illus. Notes*, p. 31.

a considerable extent forgotten by, the larger portion of Christendom; but it now formed[1] a closer alliance with the sister Churches of Ireland and Scotland. It was conscious of no submission to any foreign Church, but gazed fondly back to Jerusalem and the Holy Land rather than to Rome. It had its own Liturgy, its own customs, its own peculiar (although erroneous) cycle of computing Easter. It was orthodox in faith. It had, as we learn from Gildas, a regularly ordained Episcopate. It believed its Bishops to be the successors of the Apostles, and its priests claimed the power to bind and loose. It had societies, too, under religious vows; the services were chanted, and some of the churches contained several altars dedicated to martyrs.

It is of the greatest importance that we should gather all the information possible concerning the Church in Wales, and get as definite an idea of it as we can. There are, unfortunately, those who erroneously suppose that the link between the early British Church and the Church of England of the present day, was broken by the Saxon invasion; and that the present Church of England arose in the time of Augustine, deriving its origin from Rome through him, and not, as we are bound to maintain, from the Apostles and Jerusalem in unbroken, continuous descent, through the British or Celtic Church. Every student of history knows that the Church in Wales was in existence when Augustine arrived in England in A.D. 597. It was the remnant of the early British Church, mentioned by

---

[1] About the middle of the fifth century a combination of Churches of the British confession arose.

Tertullian as early as A.D. 200, and by Origen only a little later. The Saxon invasion had destroyed civilization and Christianity in the larger part of England proper, but a remnant was driven westward, and found its home in Wales. Augustine held two Conferences with the Bishops and clergy of this remnant of the British Church. One of these was on the banks of the Severn, at a place still known as "St. Augustine's Oak." He found " seven Bishops and a large number of learned men." In his letter to Gregory, he asked for instructions as to several particulars; one of them, "how he was to deal with the British Bishops." Dinoth told him they had "their own Archbishop at Caerleon-on-Usk," and it is well known that the British Bishops refused to unite with Augustine and the Church of the Saxons.

This independence continued long after the Saxons gained control of Wales, and it was not until the beginning of the ninth century that they conformed to the rest of the Western Church in regard to the keeping of Easter. And until a yet later period they continued to maintain their ecclesiastical independence of the Church of England. Indeed it was not until the end of the thirteenth century that the union was consummated, and Wales finally included within the province of Canterbury. It is an interesting fact, however, as illustrating the connection of the Church in Wales with that in England, that one of the Bishops appointed to the See of St. David's (1092), Hervè, or Hervæus, a Breton, having been rejected by the Welsh people (being unfamiliar with the Welsh dialect) became the first Bishop of Ely in the year A.D. 1109.

It is well to remember these facts, that we may have a clear idea of the position of the Church in Wales. From them we may see that the Welsh Church of to-day is the lineal descendant of the oldest Church in Britain. Wales received its Christianity, not from Roman Missionaries, but from the early British Church, which flourished long before Augustine was born. The present dioceses were all founded before Augustine ever set foot on British shores.[1] The property, too, or the greater part of it, has been in the possession of that Church from the earliest times. It was not seized by force or conferred by Parliament, but was bestowed upon it by kings, nobles, and landed proprietors long centuries before the Parliament of England had an exist-ence. Probably there is no other property in England that has been in the hands of the same owners so long. By no right can that property be alienated by Parlia-ment, except by the right of the stronger—a right which may be brought to bear against the property of laymen no less than against that of the Church. Let the Mem-bers of Parliament beware. "Whatsoever a man soweth, that shall he also reap."

If we have to regret that the ecclesiastical history of the fifth and sixth centuries is not so full and clear as we could wish, it must be remembered that the same is true of the civil history of the same period. Modern criticism has shown the almost impossibility of extracting trustworthy details from the confused traditions of the Saxon conquest. Even the existence of Hengist and

---

[1] According to Haddon and Stubbs (*Councils*, etc.), there is no trace in the Church of Wales of any other system than that of diocesan episcopacy.

Horsa, of Vortigern and Arthur, have been called in question. Can we wonder, then, when Christianity was so sorely persecuted, when its persecutors tried all they could to destroy all vestiges of the hated religion of a hated people, when Christianity was driven out of the best portions of the country, and forced to take refuge amongst the mountains in a remote corner of the land, that many of the memorials perished, or that the Church was well-nigh forgotten for a time? The wonder is that we have so many documents as we have. With them we must be content, and they are quite sufficient for our purpose. " There are," says Hore, " three very reliable tests of the condition of a Church: (1) its missions; (2) its colleges and schools of learning; (3) the number of its saints and holy men "; and, judged by these tests, we find that the British Church held an important position in Christendom.[1]

EMINENT MEN.

Before leaving the consideration of this period of the history of the Church, let us think of some of the great men who aided in shaping her future destiny, and making her power and influence felt both near and far.

DUBRICIUS, Dyfrig, of whom mention has already been made, was the first Bishop of Llandaff, and probably became the Archbishop of Caerleon-on-Usk. He was a man of great learning, and a natural leader

---

[1] For the *first* of these, *vide* Chap. III. ; for the *second*, see pp. 51-54 ; and for the *third*, pp. 64-72.

N.B.—These institutions of learning were of incalculable value at a later period, in furnishing missionaries to the Saxons and others—missionaries who could preach to the people in their own language.

of men. His school at Llandaff was very celebrated. He finally resigned the See, and withdrew to a monastery in the Island of Bardsey, where he died and was buried about A.D. 612. He was succeeded in the See of Llandaff by St. Teilo. In 1120 his bones were removed from Bardsey, and buried in the Cathedral of Llandaff.

ST. DAVID, the patron saint of Wales, is said to have been the son of Xantus (a prince of Wales), and uncle to King Arthur. Having been educated first at Llantwit Major, and afterwards at the College of Paulinus at Whitland, he visited Jerusalem. There he received further instruction and consecration at the hands of the Patriarch of Jerusalem. By permission of King Arthur he removed the seat of the Archbishop from Caerleon to Menevia, called after him, St. David's. He was a man of great learning and eloquence, and remarkable for the austerity of his life. He is said to have built twelve monasteries, the chief of which was at Menevia, St. David's. He died about A.D. 601.

SAMPSON, one of the scholars of Illutus, having been consecrated a Bishop at large (*sine titulo*) by Dubricius, went over to Armorica,[1] or French Britain, A.D. 522. He is said to have taken with him many of the monuments of the early British Church (several of which have been recovered), and to have become Archbishop

---

[1] Armorica (Celt.) from *ar*, on or near ; and *mor*, sea.

Brittany, on the coast of Gaul, was founded by a colony of Britons (whence its name), during the Saxon troubles, as a convenient station near to their own country, where they might receive their countrymen who were suffering from persecution, or from which they might return home if they thought fit. Hore's *Eighteen Centuries*. Note, p. 56.

of Dôl, or Dole.   In Armorica, or Brittany, many British Christians found a refuge, among whom may be named St. Malo, St. Brica, and Gildas the historian.

St. Cadoc, or Cattwg, was the son of a chieftain in Monmouthshire.   His mother is said to have been one of the children of Brychan, who gave his name to Breconshire.   He was one of the most noted men of his age; a saintly and active abbot, a prince of influence and ability, a genial and gentle sage.   He founded the monastery of Llancarvan, which occupied so distinguished a place in the movement for the revival of Irish Christianity at a later date.   Indeed he visited Ireland, and numbered Finnian of Clonard among his pupils; and a little later, Finnian became the teacher of the renowned Columba of " Iona " fame.   It follows that, if we trace our English Christianity back to the Scoto-Irish missionaries of Lindisfarne and Iona, and then follow the chain of evidence a link or two further, we shall find that we owe the Church in Wales a great debt of gratitude.   Cadoc's monastery, Llancarvan, located in the town of the same name, about twelve miles west from Cardiff,[1] became one of the three great monasteries of the See of Llandaff, Llantwit Major and Docwinni being the other two.   Here Cadoc spent several years of his life.   Such was his charity that, beside the ordinary hospitality of his table, he is said to have supported three hundred clergy and poor people out of his patrimony.   He went to Armorica (Brittany), where he remained some years, and then returned to his native land, not, however, to end his life in his monastery at

---

1 The place, like St. Asaph, however, takes its name from his successor.

Llancarvan. He now chose as the scene of his labours Weedon, in Northamptonshire. There, while celebrating the divine offices, he suffered martyrdom at the hands of the Saxons, A.D. 570.[1]

ST. PADARN, the friend of St. David, was a native of Brittany. He came over to Ireland first and then to Wales. He studied under Illtyd, at Llantwit Major, and afterwards founded a monastery and bishopric at the place called after him, Llanbadarn Fawr (the Church of Padarn the Great).[2] A church still standing there bears his name. This town of Llanbadarn Fawr was made the centre of his diocese, and so continued for many years, but it was finally absorbed in the diocese of St. David's.

ST. TEILO, a pupil of Dubricius, and the intimate friend of St. David, succeeded Dubricius as the second Bishop of Llandaff. It is reported that he was "united to St. David by so much love and the grace of the Holy Spirit, that in their deeds they both had the same

---

[1] The following quaint lines found in the writings of St. Cadoc show the respect for learning which animated the Welsh people of those early days. Of the things which are "hateful" this ancient Welsh saint tabulates :

> "A bishop without learning.
> A nation without science.
> A parish without education.
> A young man without knowledge.
> A scholar without books."

And again :

> "No teacher, no learning.
> No learning, no science.
> No science, no wisdom.
> No wisdom, no godliness.
> No godliness, no God.
> No God, nothing."

[2] In the old British or Welsh dialect P and B, as also T and D, are interchangeable where euphony requires it.

thought with respect to what was to be done and left undone." Both he and Padarn accompanied David on that pilgrimage to Jerusalem already referred to. That he was a great leader in his day is certain, from the large number of churches in the dioceses of Llandaff and St. David's which bear his name. "The Welsh branches of the Church of England Temperance Society," says Mr. Newell, "would do well to choose him as their patron, as he would seem to have been the earliest founder of their institution."

ILLTYD, or Illutus, was, most probably, a native of Brittany, and will ever be celebrated as the founder of the great school or monastery which bore his name ; for of all the old monasteries of Wales, it may well be said that none was more interesting than the college of Illtyd, at what is now called Llantwit Major.

A small, scattered village, near the shore of the Bristol Channel, now marks the place to which, in the sixth century, Illtyd and his companions retired. Newell, in his *Ancient British Church*, says, "On approaching the village the visitor sees a large ruined building, which, although comparatively modern, impresses his mind, by its size and importance, with ideas of past greatness, and prepares him for what is to succeed. Descending the hill through the quaint village of many streets, he comes to a plain ancient building with a belfry. This is now the Town Hall, and the bell still bears the inscription, '*Sancte Illute, ora pro nobis.*' Near this is the old church, a small, simple structure with little external ornament, showing by its architecture no signs of greater antiquity than the thirteenth century, yet standing, it can scarcely be doubted, on the same site as Illtyd's own church.''

The Triads reckon Llantwit in the first rank of British monasteries, and ascribe to it two thousand four hundred students. An ancient tradition, which is also affirmed by the Triads, says that the worship of God was kept up here without ceasing, the monks with the students taking the service by rotation, a hundred each hour. A busy and pious life was spent in this quiet spot by that Christian colony—a useful life too, for which the world was all the better. The fields around were cultivated by the community, or were used for the pasture of their flocks, and thus their simple wants were supplied. The waters of the Bristol Channel, which at first occasionally flooded the low-lying meadows, were kept out by an embankment. The students may not have known much about many branches taught in our modern schools, but what they studied they studied thoroughly. Gildas, who was a student here, had a very thorough acquaintance with the Bible, as his writings prove. Would that the same could be said of the students at our modern colleges. With no doubts and few cares, their lives were spent in health and happiness.

ST. KENTIGERN, popularly called Mungo (the gentle and beloved one), regarded as the son of a British prince, was born at Culross on the Forth about A.D. 514. He went to Cathures (Glasgow) and there founded a monastery, and also the See of Glasgow, of which, despite his own scruples (for he was at the time only in his twenty-fifth year) he was consecrated Bishop. His diocese, as we should say, included the kingdom of Cambria. He, St. Columba, and St. Ninian, must ever be regarded as the three great missionaries of Scotland. He was driven from his northern See by the king, Morken, and went to Menevia to St. David. On his way he tarried at Karleolum (Carlisle) winning many of the idolatrous inhabitants to the true faith. After a brief stay at St. David's he retired to North Wales, where, at the junction of the Clwyd and Elwy, he founded the Monastery of Llanelwy and also an episcopal See. Here he intended to end his days, and in death to rest in sight of the children he had begotten in the Gospel. But God's Will was otherwise. He was recalled to Scotland by Rederesh, or Rhydderch Hael, who by a successful battle had become King of the Strathclyde Britons. And warned of God in a dream St. Kentigern bade farewell to his assembled clergy and returned to his work in Scotland. He founded a church at Glasgow where the cathedral now stands. At length, full of years and blessings, he passed away from this world to his Father, in the year 612, according to the " Annales Cambriae." His tomb is still pointed out in the magnificent crypt of the cathedral which bears his name. That cathedral is famous for its preservation by the citizens of Glasgow from the destructive zeal of the Reformers.

St. Asaph, after Kentigern, whose life he wrote, must be mentioned. He was a person of noble birth, and eminent for piety and learning. He was also the friend and pupil of Kentigern, and unanimously elected to succeed him at Llanelwy. From him, its second Bishop, the Diocese of St Asaph takes its name.

DANIEL, or Deiniol Wyn, was the son of Dunawd Fawr. He founded the monastery called after him Bangor Deiniol, or sometimes Bangor Fawr, at the place which still bears the name of Bangor, and now possesses a Welsh college. He was the founder and first Bishop of the See of Bangor. His son Deiniol became abbot of the monastery after him. This monastery had great fame among the Celtic Churches. Deiniol, together with his father and his two brothers, are said to have co-operated in the establishment of the renowned monastery of Bangor Iscoed. He died A.D. 584, and was buried in the island of Bardsey.[1]

Of *SS. Ninian, Patrick, Finian, Columba, Columban,* and *Aidan,* and of their missionary enterprises, some account will be found in the next chapter. But mention must be made here of *Gildas,* the historian. He was born, according to Archbishop Usher, A.D. 522, and died 570. He was educated at the famous school of Illtyd, and became a monk at Bangor. His piety and learning were very conspicuous. Archbishop Usher thinks he wrote his work, *De Excidis Britanniac, circ.* A.D. 564. His works were well known to literary men of the seventh and eighth centuries. Six chapters of Bede's first book are almost entirely transcriptions from Gildas. Besides his extant works, Geoffrey of Monmouth speaks of a larger historical work, which apparently is lost.

---

[1] *Note.*—" The contemporaneousness of the first Bishops," says Canon Bevan, " is a noticeable fact. Deiniol is said to have died A.D. 584 ; St. David, 601 ; Kentigern and Dubricius, 612. Thus three, out of the four founders of the Welsh Sees, survived the arrival of St. Augustine."

KINDNESS OF THE MONKS TO LIVING THINGS.

Love for every living thing was, in those early times, considered as a special mark of saintliness. Illtyd is said to have protected a hunted stag, which took shelter in his cell, when pursued by the hounds of King Meirchion. It is also said that Prince Einion was one day hunting among the rocks and woods of the Wye. A wearied stag came in its flight to where Oudoceus, the Bishop of Llandaff, was. The stag lay down on his cloak near to where he was. The Bishop, pitying it, and considering that it had thus appealed to him for protection, saved it from the hunters ; and the prince, struck by the strange event, made a gift of the spot to the Bishop and Church at Llandaff. Another very touching story, illustrating the kindness of his nature, is told of St. Columba.

OUR INDEBTEDNESS TO THE MONKS OF BRITAIN.

Newell has well said that " many of the usages and opinions which we encounter," in reviewing the History of the Ancient Church of Britain, " wear to our eyes a strange and unfamiliar, perhaps at times a repellent, aspect. Yet for us the olden saints toiled and died; to us they left a heritage of Catholic truth and order, which has been handed down through successive centuries, and withal a spirit of national independence and hostility to foreign usurpation. More precious still is the legacy of their deep personal piety, their devout realization of the companionship of the Divine Master, their contempt of the world, their clear conception of the future life, in the contemplation of which they spent their days on earth; and this united with the lovable qualities that spring from the kindly Celtic heart, with love of nature, gentleness to the weak, even to animals, indignation against oppression, burning zeal for the salvation of souls, and 'the enthusiasm of humanity.' Gildas, indeed, is a stern and melancholy figure on the page of history, but his friend, the cheerful and kindly Cadoc, his tutor, Illtyd, the protector of the hunted stag, are equally representative of the Celtic monk, and, like Colomba of Iona, win our heart, while they impress our imagination and our judgment. English Churchmen may well prize the legacy such saints have left as a most precious part of their inheritance from antiquity.

"We may disapprove of monasticism without dissociating ourselves from the early monks, who were the salt of the earth. England, of all the countries of Europe 'the most deeply furroughed by the monastic plough,' should not suffer an idle prejudice to blind her to the services of her benefactors. We need not superstitiously reverence their defects; but we ought to admire their virtues. If we are ungrateful the loss is wholly ours; we suffer by losing the meaning of 'the Communion of Saints'—they, to whom in their missionary zeal 'every foreign land was their own country, and every country but a foreign land,' have now reached their true native land, the rest and peace which no ingratitude can impair.

"Yet, however successive ages may vary in regarding these early workers . . . the beautiful land of Wales, where so many of these holy men lived and died, ever recounts to the willing listener the story of the olden days. The names of its villages, of its islands, rocks, and wells—the carved and inscribed stones which are so common, keep fresh the memory of its saints and of their faith. Bardsey [1] and Llantwit may be unknown and unnoticed, but their witness is writ large for all who visit them. To parody Dr. Johnson's oft-quoted words respecting Iona :—That Welshman is little to be envied whose patriotism would not gain force or whose piety would not grow warmer among the ruins of Bardsey. But Bardsey and Llantwit are but prominent examples of what is found all over Wales. The rocky island bears the name of the hermit who made it his abode ; the sea-beaten promontory has some ruined chapel that was once a beacon to the sailor ; the enclosed valley some fragment of a monastery of ancient foundation, where the traveller over the rugged pass found shelter, rest, and food freely provided. Glamorgan, where populous river-valleys, with mines and furnaces, alternate with bleak and barren mountain-tops—where an undulating plain of luxuriant greenery slopes from breezy heights to an island-studded sea, has everywhere in the midst of its centres of population, its quiet villages, and its desolate wilds, churches which olden saints founded, crosses, stones, and wells with

---

[1] Bardsey (the island of the bards) may well be called the Iona of Wales. There Dubricius and Deiniol were buried ; thither retired the saints, after their life of conflict, to find rest and peace in prayer and meditation, with the fair prospect of Cardigan Bay before their eyes. According to a legend still preserved by a monument erected by Lord Newborough upon the island, the bodies of 20,000 Welsh saints were there laid to rest.

which their memory or their faith is in some way connected. To him who has once realized how the sacred
history of Wales is written upon its surface, more
clearly than its geological history in its rocks,[1] the
whole country wears a changed aspect, and,

> " Meadow, grove, and stream,
> The earth and every common sight,
> To *him* doth seem
> Apparell'd in celestial light."

Esto perpetua (may it live for ever) was the prayer of
Coleridge for the Church of England, and, while we join
therein, let us remember that we are praying for the
perpetuity of that Church for which St. Alban shed his
blood, for which German and Lupus fought the battle
of orthodoxy, and for which the old British saints and
worthies toiled and suffered and died.

HYMN FOR THE CHURCH IN WALES.

" The gates of Hell shall not prevail against it."

Far back in distant ages, by God's most loving Will,
The Church in Wales was planted, the Church that lives there
　　　　still;
The Church that Jesus purchased, that, being all His own,
He might present it spotless before the Father's throne.

Her Sacramental Blessings, her never-changing Creed,
Are Gifts to her from Jesus, Who owns her His indeed,
Who hath, through God the Spirit, true Source of Life Divine,
Preserved her Holy Orders in yet unbroken line.

---

[1] Baedeker's *Great Britain* gives a list of no fewer than *fifty-eight* proper names
in Wales, all beginning with the word for Church, *Llan.*

The Church fights on undaunted, for Christ her Living Head
Of His own mystic Body hath words of promise said,
How 'gainst its Rock Foundation all power of evil fails,
And on that Rock of Ages is built the Church in Wales.

Stand firm then fellow Churchmen; we are not left alone,
The Christ Who died to save us is watching from His Throne,
And as He pleads unceasing His Sacrifice above,
We make the same great Offering in Eucharists of Love.

In union with His pleading for ever doth arise,
A stream of Intercession from those in Paradise
Who, since the Gospel message first reached our shores of old,
Have lived and died for Jesus within the Church's Fold.

So worshipping the Father, the Spirit, and the Son,
Unswerving faith confessing in God the Three in One,
The Church on earth still fighting, the Church at rest above,
Is ever safely guarded by God's eternal love.   Amen.

G. H.

Esto Perpetua.

CHAPTER III.

THE MISSIONARY CHARACTER AND WORK OF THE EARLY BRITISH CHURCH.

SAXONS, JUTES, AND ANGLES ; NO EFFORTS MADE FOR THEIR CONVERSION. REASON GIVEN—MARRIAGE OF ETHELBERT AND BERTHA PROVIDENTIALLY OPENS THE WAY—MISSIONARY WORK OF THE BRITISH CHURCH : ST. NINIAN, ST. PATRICK, ST. PATRICK AND THE CHURCH OF IRELAND, ST. FINNIAN OF COLONARD, ST. FINNIAN OF MOYVILLE, ST. COLUMBA AND IONA, HIS TRAINING AT MOYVILLE AND COLONARD, HIS WORK IN IRELAND, STORY OF HIS EXILE, LANDS AT IONA AND MAKES THE PLACE RENOWED, HIS HEROIC LABOURS, NOT A ROMAN CATHOLIC—MONASTIC SYSTEM, NO ARGUMENT FOR PARITY AFFORDED—INDEBTEDNESS OF THE CHURCH IN IRELAND TO THE BRITISH CHURCH, MISSIONARY ENTHUSIASM—-IRISH SAINTS, PATRONS OR FOUNDERS—ST. COLUMBAN, WORK OF—BRITISH CHURCH NEGLECTED THE SAXONS—ST. AIDAN, APOSTLE OF ENGLAND—THE CHURCH PLANETS OF BRITAIN.

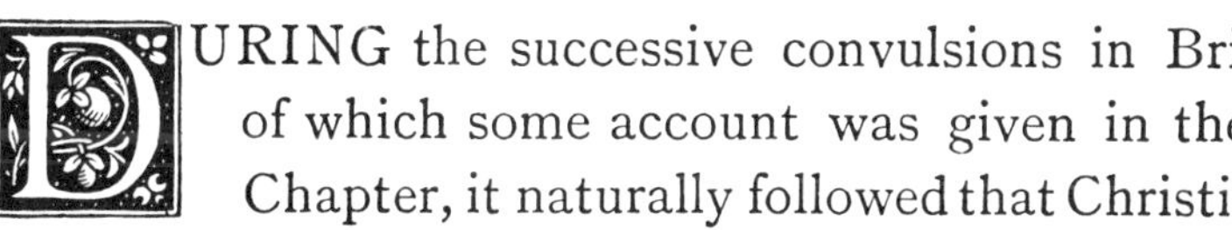

DURING the successive convulsions in Britain, of which some account was given in the last Chapter, it naturally followed that Christianity found but little encouragement in the midst of elements so uncongenial. The Saxons, Jutes, and Angles being pagans to a man, and having treated the Christians so cruelly, were not very likely soon to see efforts made by the British clergy for their conversion ; neither was it probable, had such efforts been made, that these Saxon masters would have embraced the Gospel at the hands of those whom they so much despised. This deplorable disposition, on both sides, to stand apart each from the other, might long have continued, had not the marriage of Ethelbert, King of Kent, with Bertha, daughter of Charibert, a Frankish King, of Paris, providentially paved the way for Ethelbert's conversion to the Christian Faith.   This pagan king, " under the designation of *Bretwalda,* enjoyed an admitted precedence over the other Anglo-Saxon potentates," [1] and extended his kingdom to the Humber.   Charibert would not consent to the marriage of his daughter to a pagan, until the free exercise of her religion was guaranteed by the Saxon, and the attendance of a Christian Bishop, *Luidhard,* as her chaplain, agreed to.   On these conditions Bertha became his wife in A.D. 570,[2] and came to Canterbury.[3]   On the chalk downs, overlooking the valley of the Stour, close by, there stood a little church, which had been built some time before by British Christians, and had by them been named after St. Martin. Though well-nigh a ruin, it was speedily restored and devoted to her use ; and we may well believe that Queen Bertha, on arriving from France, was delighted to find that the church in which she was to worship had long before been called after the great saint of her own land ; for even before the Saxon invasion that name had become so famous that many churches were called after him.[4]   Here, then, in the very headquarters

---

[1] Soames' *Anglo-Saxon Church*, p. 23.

[2] Authors differ as to this date, some putting the marriage as late as from 583 to 589.

[3] To his credit be it recorded that Ethelbert faithfully performed all that he promised, both in its letter and in its spirit.

[4] *St. Martin's* Church at Canterbury still stands, a monument of early British Christianity.   We have the testimony of the Venerable Bede that there was on this spot a " church built while the Romans inhabited Britain " ; and the

of the Saxon dominion, a Christian congregation assembled; and here the young Queen acquired such an ascendency over Ethelbert, that we may well believe he was easily reconciled to the efforts she made to win her adopted countrymen to the Christian Faith; and it cannot be doubted that she did much, at a later period, to induce him to receive favourably Augustine and his monks, of whose mission account will be given in the next Chapter.

Special attention should be directed to this historical fact, viz., that the British Church was not derived from that of Rome. It existed independently of the Church in Italy down to the close of the sixth century, bound to it only by friendship and amity, as it was to all the other parts of the Church Catholic. It owed no subjection whatever to any foreign power, nor is there a record of any Roman ecclesiastic claiming any such subjection down to the close of the sixth century.

present outside walls abound in Roman bricks; but it was not supposed, until quite recently, that any of the original church was left *in situ*, except a portion of the wall on the South side of the chancel. When, however, in making repairs, a few years ago, they took down a portion of the woodwork at the South-east side of the nave (for the purpose of the better uncovering of the Norman piscina), and the whitewash was scraped off, parts of an old wall were exposed to view. This wall was built of stone and rubble, with regular bonding courses of Roman brick at intervals, and it was found to be faced with Roman plaster. Panels were taken out in different parts of the nave, and the same wall was found with fragments of the same facing. This Roman wall has been traced five feet from the ground, and most probably it extends a great deal higher; but it was not thought expedient to proceed further at the time with the investigation, as it would have necessitated an interruption of the Church Services. We may therefore conclude that the persons who compose the congregations of the present day at St. Martin's are actually worshipping in the original British Church, within the very same walls which were sanctified by the prayers of Queen Bertha, and afterwards by the preaching of Augustine.

MISSIONARY WORK.

But though the British Church did not make efforts for the conversion of the pagan Saxons, it must not be inferred that she was destitute of a missionary spirit. Such was not the case. The great glory of the British Church consisted in her Missionary enterprises, which caused her name to be regarded with reverence, in the sixth and seventh centuries, by Christians of every grade throughout the whole North-western part of the Continent of Europe. From the middle of the fifth century the name of British or Celtic Churches comprised not only the Christians of Wales, but also the Irish or Scots, and the Caledonians.[1] To make this the more intelligible it will be necessary to form a correct idea as to the origin of these sister Churches of the British confession.

Let it be remembered, then, that the early inhabitants of Ireland were Scots. "It is probable," says Gibbon, "that in some remote period of antiquity the fertile plains of Ulster received a colony of hungry Scots; . . . it is certain that in the declining age of the Roman Empire, Caledonia, Ireland, and the Isle of Man were inhabited by Scots."[2] Hence Ireland was generally called "Scotia," or "Insulæ Scotorum," by the the writers of the sixth and seventh centuries ; and the name of Scotland, as applied to the Northern part of Britain (which was at

---

[1] Hook, I., 10.   Under the name "Britannicæ Insulæ" the ancients included Albion or England, Scotland, and Hibernia or Ireland, and the adjacent islands. "The Irish Churches," says Soames, "might be connected, as are the Church of England and the Episcopal Church of North America."

[2] *Decline and Fall*, Vol. IV., p. 294.

that time inhabited solely by the Picts) is of comparatively modern date. In process of time the Scots, migrating from Ireland under Penda, their leader, either by fair means or by force of arms, secured to themselves those settlements amongst the Picts which they still possess. For a time the two peoples answered to the division of Highlanders and Lowlanders of modern times; but by degrees the Scots gained on and subdued the Picts, so that in the ninth century they became supreme, and gave their name to the country.

St. Ninian. During the early part of the fifth century, *St. Ninian*, the son of a British chief, preached the Gospel to the Southern Picts, a people of whom it was said "that they had more hair on their faces than clothes on their bodies." He had received much of his education in Gaul, and was consecrated Bishop by the renowned St. Martin, of Tours. He founded *Whitherne*, or *Whiteherne*, near the mouth of the Clyde, and made that the head of his See. Here he built a church of white stone, and dedicated it to St. Martin. It received the name of "Candida Casa,"[1] a name afterwards given to the See. After eight years of successful missionary effort he was compelled by the violence of barbarian hordes to leave his work and take refuge in Ireland.

St. Patrick. About the year A.D. 432 Patrick, afterwards known as St. Patrick, went into Ireland, and established Christianity in the country. He was so successful in his work that he has been called ever since the "Apostle of Ireland."

[1] The remains of this once celebrated church may still be seen. It was undoubtedly the first church in the British Islands that had been built of stone, and so it marks a new era in the church architecture of the country.

This great man, whose original name was Succoth, but to whom that of Patricius or Patrick was given on account of his noble birth, was undoubtedly born near Dumbarton on the Clyde, in a village called after him Kirkpatrick. His father was a deacon and his grandfather a priest, both of St. Ninian's Mission, and his mother is believed to have been the sister of St. Martin.[1]

When he was sixteen years old a band of pirates, from the North of Ireland, landed at the mouth of the Clyde, and carried him off to Ireland, where, as a slave for six years, he was made to attend cattle. At the end of these years he managed to escape. He then went to Gaul, and studied theology in the School of St. German, Bishop of Auxerre, and probably in that of his uncle of Tours also. He was almost assuredly ordained deacon and priest by St. German, and consecrated Bishop by the said German, assisted by the far-famed St. Martin. He now felt himself called to go to the land of his captivity, and preach the Gospel to the Irish.

We are sometimes told that Pope Celestine ordained Palladius (who was a Briton) a deacon, and sent him into Ireland before St. Patrick entered on his work there. Very true, Palladius did go to Ireland about the year 430, but his mission proved a complete failure, and he was expelled from the country by the King of Leinster, and died shortly after.[2] Not, then, to Palladius but to St. Patrick belongs the honour of the

---

[1] This information as to his parentage is given by himself in his " Confessions." As to the place of his birth, he mentions it as being "*in Britanniis.*"

[2] That there were Christians in Ireland even before Palladius is shown by Haddon and Stubbs' " Councils and Ecclesiastical Documents," Vol. II., Part II., p. 288.

conversion of Ireland. His mission was eminently successful, one of his first converts being the King himself. With true devotion he preached the Gospel from North to South. He is said to have built about 360 churches, to have baptized 12,000 converts, and to have ordained many Deacons, Priests, and Bishops.[1] He fixed his principal See at Armagh, A.D. 454, and that has continued to be the seat of the Primate of the Church of Ireland. He lived to see the whole country Christianized, and after a long and useful career he, according to Archbishop Usher, fell asleep in the year A.D. 493, at the age of 120 years.

There is a curious contrast between St. Patrick's name and his *first* Irish expedition. His name means patrician, and his life there for six years was that of a slave.

This appears to be a suitable place for emphasizing a few facts concerning *St. Patrick and the Irish Church*, about which there is a lamentable lack of information.

1. Do the thousands of Roman Catholics, and especially Irish Roman Catholics, who join so heartily in the celebration of St. Patrick's Day, and sound his praises so loudly, realize that *he never was a Roman Catholic?* This fact is overlooked, or not understood, by many others who do not belong to the Roman obedience. Romanists claim him, and many who protest against Rome, weakly and ignorantly give up to Roman monopolization one who never owed or acknowledged allegiance either to the Bishop or Church of Rome. What has the Church, whose boast is *semper idem*, to

---

[1] The Isle of Man, too, is said to have received its first Bishop from St. Patrick about A.D. 447. Churton, *Anc. Brit. Ch.*, 19.

say as to his parentage ? Deacons and priests in that Church are not supposed to have sons. His own account of his parentage, given in his " Confessions," reveals to us the fact that the domestic and social life of the clergy of his day was very much like that of the clergy of the Church of Ireland, or of the Church of England, of our day, and very unlike that of the clergy of the Roman obedience in modern times.

Moreover, he received his orders not from Rome, but from the *Gallican* Church (as did also St. Augustine, of a later period), which Church derived its existence from St. John, and Irenæus, and Ephesus, and was as independent of Rome as the Church of England or the Church of Ireland is to-day.

He never held or taught the modern doctrines of the Immaculate Conception and Papal Infallibility. Both have been invented and promulgated in our times, to wit, in 1854 and 1870 respectively. His teaching was in harmony with primitive Christianity, with the Apostles' and Nicene Creeds, which until this day are held and taught by the Church of Ireland, which he founded. As to the Creed of Pope Pius IV.—the Official Creed of the Church of Rome—neither St. Patrick nor any other person had ever seen or heard of it in his day; and we believe, and are sure, that if he were now living in the Roman communion, and held and taught the very same doctrines which he held and taught in Ireland in the fifth century, he would be promptly excommunicated for heresy. But he would find that the Church, which he founded in Ireland, had " kept the Faith."

2. The Church of Ireland—and by this title is meant the same Church which in England is called the Church of England—is the legitimate successor and representative of that ancient Church established in Ireland more than 1,400 years ago by St. Patrick, and to her the title of "Church of Ireland" legitimately belongs. It owns and occupies the Cathedral of Armagh, which stands on the very spot where St. Patrick built his chief or principal church. Armagh was his principal diocese, and the Most Rev. Dr. Alexander, who was elevated to that primatial See a short time ago, is his legitimate successor in office. The Cathedral in Dublin also, which bears his name, although not built by him, stands on the site of an abbey which he erected in A.D. 450. This, too, is the property of the Church of Ireland, and has been through all the centuries down to the present day.

Lord Plunket, the late Archbishop of Dublin, in an eloquent sermon delivered recently before an Irish Synod, used the following language:—"I cannot forget that those whom I address are members of the Church of Ireland. Surely, if love of your country, and pride in her ancient traditions should burn brightly in any hearts, it should do so in yours. You belong to a communion which claims, and, as I believe, rightly claims, to be the representative and successor in this land *of Ireland's ancient Church*. That ancient Church was an Episcopal Church. It was, moreover, an independent Church, holding its own Synods, electing its own Bishops, and *owing no allegiance to any foreign control*. The only religious body in Ireland that now combines these distinctive characteristics is our own. Nor is this all. Our Bishops can, as I firmly believe, trace their lineage . . . by the historic continuity of a duly ordained succession, to the Irish Episcopate of the far-off past. I say this, not in any spirit of arrogant boasting, or ungenerous rivalry towards our brethren of the various Protestant bodies in this land. I honour them for their works' sake. But they will not, I am sure, respect me the less because I give expression to the honest convictions of my mind. And as a patriot, who desires to awaken a spirit of patriotism in my fellow-churchmen's hearts, I should be untrue to those convictions were I not to remind you of the glorious days when the Church to which you now belong evangelized the dark places of Christendom, and won for Ireland the proud title of the ' Isle of Saints.' "

3. As to the Church of Rome in Ireland (a modern " Italian Mission " in Ireland as well as in England), every scholar of history knows that it derives its orders from Bishops introduced into that country—some from Spain and some from Italy—in the sixteenth century. They went there under instructions from Pope Pius IV., and were placed in Sees already occupied by Irish Bishops. There is not a Bishop of the Roman obedience in Ireland to-day who will attempt to claim, in the face of the facts of history, that he has received his orders or consecration in succession from St. Patrick. The Bishops of the Church of Ireland, however, can and do make this claim, and it cannot be disproved. Be it remembered, then, that the present Church of Ireland, and not the Roman sect introduced there in

A.D. 1565, is the continuation of the ancient Catholic Church of the land, founded by St. Patrick more than a thousand years earlier.

4. From the days of St. Patrick to the conquest of Ireland by Henry II., in 1172, the Irish Church enjoyed a complete autonomy, and was free from all foreign control. It governed itself, knew no superior to its own Episcopate, and acknowledged no more obedience to Rome than to any other diocese in Christendom. During these centuries it was illuminated by learning, piety, and zeal. Its schools were frequented by students from various parts of Europe. Its teachers were eminent for their great piety and self-denial, and its missionaries carried the Gospel to many parts of the Continent, where their labours were crowned with success and benediction. Through all this period, when the Church of Rome had scarcely anything to do with Ireland, Christianity flourished as it has never done since the Popes have had to do with that island.

5. The question naturally arises—*How and when was Romanism introduced into Ireland?* First, through the influence and connection of the Danes with Ireland. The Danes, who invaded and pillaged Ireland, settled in Dublin, Limerick, and Waterford. They afterwards became converted to Christianity; but as they claimed affinity with the Normans they got their Bishops from Canterbury. Lanfranc and Anselm were partisans of Rome, and were thus *the first* to gain a foothold in Ireland for papal pretensions, near the close of the eleventh century. The Bishop of Limerick was nominated by the Pope as his legate in 1106, and in 1151 the

Pope, for the first time, sent the pall as a present to the four Archbishops. All the while, however, there was but one Church in Ireland, viz., the old Church of the land, but now becoming more and more Romanised.

Then, in 1156, Henry II., of England, applied to the Pope, Nicholas Brakespeare (the son of a priest at St. Alban's, and the only English Pope), known as Adrian IV., for permission to take possession of Ireland, and to make himself and his successors, the kings of England, masters of it; in order, he said, to establish religion "*in its purity*"—showing that the religion which was there already, was not, in his estimation, all that it ought to be; in other words, it was not under the control of the Bishop of Rome. The Pope granted Henry's request, under the pretence that "all islands" had been given to the Popes by the so-called "Donation of Constantine," and issued his bull accordingly.[1] If it be asked why the Pope sanctioned Henry's invasion of Ireland, the answer is given in his own bull: "To widen the bounds of the Church, and to extend her jurisdiction *where she has none at present*." The Pope exacted a further condition, that the English King should pay him "a penny a year for every inhabited house in the island," thus furnishing the evidence that "Peter's pence" had not hitherto been paid from the Church in Ireland.

It will be seen that the transaction, on the part of the Roman Pontiff at least, was of the most deliberate and

---

[1] *Vide* Dr. Lanigan's *Eccles. Hist. of Ireland* (4 vols., 1822). Also Abbé Fleury's *Histoire Ecclesiastique* (20 vols.). Both of these were Roman Catholic priests; the former was born at Cashel, in 1758.

carefully calculated kind. It is a little marvellous that Romanists of to-day in Ireland are so ill at ease under English rule. They ought to know that the right of England over Ireland was derived from the pretended prerogative of their own infallible Adrian IV. And that that claim was afterwards confirmed by Alexander III.

Henry, under various pretexts, with the sanction and approval of the Pope, took his armies to Ireland. The Irish chiefs, taken singly, soon submitted to him, and paid him homage. The Bishops agreed to an ecclesiastical union with the Church of England. Then Henry, to suit his own ends, handed over the Irish Church to the Pope of Rome. By these unwarranted acts schism was introduced, and Bishops and priests were appointed by order of the Pope. A few of the Bishops still continued to assert an independent position, and offered here and there a spasmodic resistance, but the independence of the Celtic Church was gone. She had been betrayed by the King of England and the Pope of Rome. Irish national independence, and Irish ecclesiastical independence terminated practically together, and in both cases by fraud and grasping usurpation. Their fate was sealed when Gelasius, Archbishop of Armagh, visited Dublin in 1172, and made his formal submission to King Henry II. From this date to the Reformation the papacy held sway, and the history of the 350 years which followed the Synod of Cashel— when the Irish Church agreed to an ecclesiastical union with the English, which at that time was permeated with Romanism—is indeed a dreary one. The Church of St. Patrick held out against a foreign usurper longer than any other Church in Western Europe, and its final submission was largely secured through the influence of the Church of England, which had to a great extent yielded already. That usurped authority was rejected and thrown off in the year 1558, after only 400 years' subjection.

6. When the work of Reformation began in England it made itself felt in Ireland also, and Protestants arrayed against Rome increased everywhere. In the reign of Edward VI. (1551) a Synod of Irish Bishops adopted the English Liturgy instead of the Latin Service Book. In 1558 the Church in Ireland united with the Church in England in accepting the reforms proposed in the reign of Queen Elizabeth, and in 1560-61 regular Synods of the Irish Bishops were held, and the Reformed English Liturgy was fully accepted. Twenty Bishops thus renounced the usurpations of the Pope and took the oaths of conformity; and from these Bishops, whose legitimate succession from St. Patrick cannot be disproved, the present Church of Ireland secures her continuity. All the Irish Bishops took the oath of supremacy except two, and they were deprived of their Sees on account of their refusal, and their adherence to the Man on the Tiber. These two were the Bishops of Meath and Kildare, and it is interesting to note that they were both intruders, put into dioceses from which the lawful Bishop had been ejected in Mary's reign. The twenty Bishops above referred to (that is to say, all the Irish Bishops except the two who had been deprived) were present at the Irish Parliament in 1559-60, when acts were passed for " restoring to the Crown its ancient

jurisdiction," and for "uniformity in religious worship." The Romanists went out of the Irish Church in 1558, and formed a new sect, securing Bishops, as has been said, from Spain and from Italy. Such is the origin of the present Italian-Spanish Mission in Ireland. These are facts which defy successful contradiction. It follows, therefore, that the *Old* Church is the Church of Ireland; the *New* Church is the Church of Rome in Ireland, which, it will be seen, has no connection with the old Church of the land—the Church of St. Patrick—but it is a foreigner, an alien, an exotic.

7. The Irish Church was despoiled of her *tithes* by the Irish Parliament in 1735, and in 1869 the English Parliament, under the lead of Mr. Gladstone, brought about her disestablishment, and largely robbed her of her *endowments.* Yet in the face of all her difficulties she still survives. " The gates of hell have not prevailed against her." Rome calls her schismatical, but history shows that it is the Church of Rome that is in schism, in Ireland as well as in England. She stole into the Irish Church in the days of Henry II. by means of schism, and she went out of it at the Reformation and set up a schism in opposition to it.

If only the brave, warm-hearted peasantry of Ireland would make themselves acquainted with the religious history of the country, and see how completely they have been imposed upon (in being deprived of their ancient rights and liberties) by the usurpations and pretentions of the occupants of the Vatican, they would rise in their might, and indignantly demand for Ireland " Home Rule " in ecclesiastical affairs, and sweep the aliens, who deprive them of local autonomy in their Church affairs, from their island.

8. The Reformation reversed the legislation of the Synod of Cashel and abolished the supremacy of the Pope. Then the Reformed Liturgy superseded that introduced at said Synod; and, at a much later period, the Act of Disestablishment swept away, with the endowments, the last remnant of that legislation. " Whatever opinions may be entertained of the Act which so many regard as unjust and sacrilegious, it has, at any rate, restored the Church of Ireland to her original freedom. She now has, as before the Anglo-Norman conquest, her own Liturgy. Her tithes have ceased, and she is maintained, as in her early days, by the voluntary contributions of her members. She is governed by her own Synods of clergy and laity, and, as of old, the " Men of Ireland " take their part in them. Now, as before the Synod of Kells, she has two Arch-bishops—one for the North, and the other for the South—and she knows no earthly authority in spiritual matters beyond the shores of Ireland. The ancient sites of churches, and the church lands granted to her by pious donors before Dane or Norman set foot in Ireland, are hers by universal admission, taken away for a time, indeed, but restored to her as the rightful owner with the full consent of all parties in the legislature, and she has resumed her ancient title of the "Church of Ireland."

Disestablishment was a heavy blow; many thought it a fatal one, and believed that the Church had fallen, never to rise again. But those evil days have passed, and the Church has learned how to accommodate her-self to her changed relations. Prejudice against her still exists, and many of the Irish people, being ignorant of her history, are unable to discern her true character and rightful claims to their allegiance. But the time will assuredly come when the masses of the people, acquainting themselves with her history, will recognize her divine mission and historic claims, and will return to her, their Mother, "as doves to their windows," and see that by her the pure Word of God is preached and the Sacraments duly administered, according to Christ's ordinance.[1]

St. Finnian. For a time, after the death of St. Patrick, the work in Ireland greatly declined, principally for want of a suitable leader. But it was reinvigorated and con-tinued by *St. Finnian*, who had been trained at St. David's monastery in Wales, and was his warm and intimate friend. He went to Ireland " to restore the faith which had fallen into neglect, and to gather together a people acceptable to the Lord." He founded the renowned monastery of Colonard, and became " the foster-father of the saints of Ireland," and the trainer and educator of those who were called " the Twelve Apostles of Ireland."[2]

There was another Finnian, of Moyville, the most noted among the students of Whitherne. He came to

---

[1] These last two paragraphs have been adapted from Tolden's *Church of Ireland*, pp. 403, 404.

[2] Among these were *St. Columba* of Iona ; Brendan, who is said to have gathered around him 3,000 disciples at Clonfret ; and Ciaran, " the son of the artificer," who founded in A.D. 548 the Monastery Clonmacnois. *Vide* Newell's *Ancient British Church*, p. 137.

Whitherne when a youth, and tradition says of him that he " first brought the Gospel to Ireland," by which is probably meant St. Jerome's translation of the Gospel.

ST. COLUMBA.   In the century following that in which St. Patrick lived and laboured, Ireland was able to pay back to Scotland the great debt she owed for St. Patrick in the person of St. Columba.   This renowned saint and missionary was born at Gartan, in the County of Donegal, A.D. 521.   He belonged to the clan which gave its name to the district, and was of the family of the Dalriad kings, to which had also belonged Milcher, St. Patrick's master.   Since St. Patrick's time the Dalriads had made a settlement on the opposite coast of Scotland, and we read of St. Columba's cousins among the chieftains there.   His mother's name was Eithne.   She was of Leinster, and of the family of a king or chieftain.   He was baptized at Temple Douglas, and received two names, which, Professor G. T. Stokes says, are " much opposed in meaning, and very significant of the contrasts and conflicts in his character—*Crimthann*, a wolf; and *Colum*, a dove."   After his baptism he was for a time committed to the care of the priest who baptized him.

From this home, where he received fostering care, he was sent to *Moyville*, a monastery in Down, on Loch Strangford, where he studied under Finnian, the lesser. There he was ordained deacon.   From Moyville he went to the monastery of *Colonard*, in Leinster, where he received further training from the greater Finnian, its founder.   At Colonard he was ordained priest by Bishop Etchen.   It will be seen, then, that by his training under

Finnian of Moyville, and Finnian of Colonard, he became the spiritual offspring both of Whitherne and of Wales—of St. Ninian's and St. David's monasteries. When he was in his twenty-third year, "Yellow Plague" scattered the community at Colonard, and he went northward. The next nineteen years were spent in ceaseless activity. He is said to have founded more than thirty monasteries, aided, no doubt, by his kinship with many of the chieftains and kings. His monastic life never severed him from the ties of clan and family. Indeed, the Irish monastic communities seem to have been incorporated with the clans, the dignity of Abbot frequently descending in the family of the founder. The communities seem, in many cases, to have consisted of a religious house, with a large outer circle of tenants, workmen, and followers, like the household of a chieftain, more or less connected by the ties of blood. Columba was not a foreigner, like St. Patrick. He dwelt among his own people, and had a passionate attachment to his country, and to his family and clan. Deeply interested in the politics of his race, tenderly clinging to early associations, bound up heart and soul with the monasteries where he had studied, reverenced as a saint, and lovingly followed by the communities which he had founded, it must have seemed as if no son of Erin was more irrevocably fixed to her soil than Columba. And yet the great work of his life was to be done elsewhere—the work which made his life a fountain of religion and civilization to the world.

The curious story as to the cause of Columba's banishment is at least characteristic of him in two particulars—his love of learning, and his dominant, fiery zeal. He was a great student, and fond of copying and possessing manuscripts. His friend, St. Finnian, of Moyville, the story relates, possessed a Psalter, which Columba greatly desired to transcribe, but Finnian not being willing for him to do so, he copied it secretly. Finnian found this out, and then claimed that the copy belonged to him as well as the Psalter. They both agreed to leave it to the decision of Diarmid, Chief or King of the Southern branch of Columba's clan, to arbitrate between them. His decision, which has become proverbial, was against Columba—" To every cow her calf; to every book its copy." This decision, we are told, angered Columba greatly, for the grudging of books was to him at all times hateful.

He was again angered when the King put to death a young prince of Connaught, who had fled to Columba for sanctuary, and claimed his protection from punishment for an involuntary murder. He executed his vengeance by stirring up the chieftains of his own tribe and of the Connaught clans to a destructive war, in which many persons were killed. " When this fit of vengeance had passed he was overwhelmed with remorse, alike by the accusations of his own conscience and by the judgment of his superiors, and set himself to do and to bear a double penace ; first, of exile from his beloved country ; and next, of converting to Christianity a number of Pagans equal to the number of Christians who had been slain in the battle. To this he consecrated his life with a reality and an intenseness which, even when we have discarded the extravagant stories of his career, win for him a glorious title of honour in the roll of the greatest missionaries of the world."

He was Abbot of Durrough, one of St. Patrick's monasteries, and forty-two years of age, when, in A.D. 563, he crossed to Scotland in a frail boat covered with ox-hides, taking with him twelve companions. They first landed, we are told, on the island of Oronsay. There, it is said, he climbed a hill, and finding he could still see the shores of Ireland, either because he did not trust himself within sight of his beloved country, or feeling that he must entirely separate himself from it, he re-embarked and landed on the island of *Iona*. It would be difficult to imagine anything more bleak and barren than this little sandy, rocky strip of flat, treeless earth was at the time. Pasture for flocks and crops for men must have been the result of severe and constant toil. And yet that island became the centre of probably the most wide-spread and most deeply-rooted missionary enterprise that the Christian world has ever known. No one who visits it can fail to appreciate the fitness of Johnson's language when he says of it, " We are now treading that illustrious island which was once the luminary of the Caledonian regions, whence savage clans and roving barbarians derived the benefit of knowledge and the blessing of religion. That man is little to be envied whose patriotism would not be strengthened upon the plain of Marathon, or whose piety would not grow warmer among the ruins of Iona."

Till this day a halo from Columba's magic name hangs over it like a spell. All has greatly changed since his day, but the island and the ruins remain to proclaim the story of his life, his missionary journeys, and his death. The tombs of the kings tell of the wide-spread fame of sanctity, which induced Sovereigns from near and far to choose it as a place of burial. Duncan among the rest, who was murdered by Macbeth, and of whom Shakespeare says that he "was carried to Colmes Kill, the sacred storehouse of his predecessors, and guardian of their bones."

Two crosses, which have survived the barbarous prejudices of Christian men, are still to be seen. One of them, McLean's Cross, is named by Adamnan, in his Life of Columba, as associated with the place where the saint rested on the last day of his life, and where the old horse of the monastery, as legend has it, came to him weeping. But perhaps the spot where one is more intensely thrilled with the power of his remarkable life than any other, is the hill which he climbed, with so much difficulty, that Saturday night, that he might have a final view of all the fields before his departure. Here it was that he delivered his latest prophecy, saying, "To this spot, although small and mean, shall come not only kings and people of the Scots, but the rulers of barbarous and remote nations with their people." Thousands of pilgrims since his day have fulfilled this prophecy and are still fulfilling it.

From that hill he went to the monastery, where he could write only part of the verse of the Psalter he was copying, "They that seek the Lord shall want no manner of thing that is good." The next morning, Sunday, June the 9th, A.D. 597, he hastened, before the other monks, to the Church, where he departed this

life before the Altar, surrounded by his spiritual children, who had hastened to him in the dim light of the
early morn to get his parting blessing. The voice was
gone, and the right hand had no longer the power to
lift itself. But raised by another, he made with it the
sign of our redemption, and with a benediction in his
heart he passed from earth to receive the benediction
of his God.

His heroism, self-denial, and devotion to his work
for Christ, may well be classed among the mightiest
records of missionary adventure that the world has ever
seen. He founded fifty-three churches and monasteries, of which traces have come down to us, in the
country now called Scotland. Thirty-two of these were
in the Western Isles, and twenty-one in the Northern
country of Caledonia, which till his day was occupied
by savage Picts. Many of the Picts had been won to
Christ by St. Ninian, but after his death had lapsed
into their former life and habits. Columba, at the risk
of his life, went to their king, *Brude*, at Inverness, with
a strong faith and steady purpose of converting him to
the Christian Faith. And in this, as indeed in so many
of his heroic ventures for Christ and the souls of men,
his efforts were crowned with success. With the conversion of the king followed the conversion of thousands
of Picts, a rich harvest of souls. He was an ideal
missionary, a man on fire with missionary zeal. When
he went to Iona, he hoped to be spared to spend thirty
years for the conversion of the Picts. And he was
spared to spend more than thirty in constant labours
night and day, toiling up and down mountain paths,

braving the perils of rocky channels and stormy seas, in journeyings often on land and sea, among the islands of the Hebrides, through Argyle and the Northern Highlands, besides his frequent returns to Ireland to strengthen and build up his beloved communities there. Though descended from chieftains, he shared in all kinds of manual labour with his fellow monks. He ground the corn with the rest, and with them engaged in the toils of agriculture and in the perils of navigation. Iona became an oasis, a focal point of heavenly light to the regions round about. For more than the third of a century he was its guiding star, reflecting the light that shone on him from the Sun of Righteousness. It became under him, and for two centuries continued to be, " the nursery of Bishops, the centre of education, the asylum of religious knowledge, the point of union among the British Isles, the capital and necropolis of the Celtic race." It became also the parent of many other religious centres. To it and to Columba not only Scotland, but the greater part of England also, owes its conversion from Paganism. Columba rested from his labours on that June morning, but his work went on, and to-day it would be impossible to estimate the posthumous results. But "the day shall declare it." "In the morning sow thy seed." He sowed the Word of Life as he went forth with his companions preaching the Gospel of peace to rude and untutored tribes, and he also reaped a rich harvest as the " laden souls of thousands meekly stealing " turned their weary steps to the kind Shepherd. What an incentive to missionary enthusiasm does his life afford ! What a reward awaits faithful, persevering toil in the Master's cause !

> " Lone Isle, though storms have round thy turrets rode,
>   Thou wert the Temple of the living God,
>   And taught earth's millions at His shrine to bow,
>   Though desolation wraps thy glories now,
>   Still thou wilt be a marvel through all time
>   For what thou hast been ; and the dead who rest
>   Around the fragments of thy walls sublime,
>   Once taught the world and harbour'd many a guest,
>   And ruled the warriors of each northern clime,
>   Thou'rt in the world like some benighted one,
>   Home of the mighty that have passed away :
>   Hail ! sainted Isle ; thou art a holy spot
>   Engraved on many hearts ; and thou art worth
>   A pilgrimage, for glories long gone by,
>   Thou noblest College of all the ancient earth,
>   Virtue and Truth, Religion itself shall die
>   Ere thou canst perish from the chart of fame,
>   Or darkness shroud the halo of thy name." [1]

It ought also to be noted that, while Columba recognized the three Orders of the Ministry and followed *Catholic* usages, he was entirely free from the accretions of later superstitions. He knew no special cult of the Blessed Virgin Mary, allowed no *supremacy* to the Bishop of Rome, and held no such dogmas as the Immaculate Conception of the Virgin Mary and the Infallibility of the Pope. In short, he was not a Roman Catholic, and knew nothing of the arrogant claims of modern Romanism.

Once more, the organization of the monastic system for the missionary work of those times, and the power

------

[1] D. Moore.

of the Abbots in the government of the communities, have given speciousness to an argument for a Presbyterian form of government, which is utterly unfounded. That there was a certain antagonism between Monks and Bishops may be conceded, as also a rivalry between Bishops and Deans in some of the Cathedrals of old foundation. But nothing stands out more clearly in ancient story than the great number of Bishops, the recognition of the Diocesan Episcopate, and the conferring of holy Orders as *the exclusive function and prerogative of the Episcopate.* The story of St. Patrick's consecrations furnishes evidence as to the number of Bishops; and the titles of the British Bishops, who attended the Council at Arles, afford proof of Diocesan Episcopacy. Let us look for a moment at the monasteries, and see in what relation Bishops stood to them. Skene says,[1] " The monastic character of the Church gave a peculiar stamp to her missionary work, which caused her to set about it in a mode well calculated to impress a people still to a great extent under the influence of heathenism. It is difficult for us now to realize to ourselves what such pagan life really was—its hopeless corruption, its utter disregard of the sanctity of domestic ties, its injustice and selfishness, its violent and bloody character ; and these characteristics would not be diminished in a people who had been partially Christianized, and had fallen back from it into heathenism. The monastic missionaries did not commence their work, as the earlier secular Church would have done, by arguing against their idolatry, superstition and

[1] *Celtic Churches.*

immorality, and preaching a purer faith : but they opposed to it the antagonistic characteristics and purer life of Christianity. They asked and obtained a settlement in some small and valueless island. There they settled down as a little Christian colony, living under a monastic rule requiring the abandonment of all that was attractive in life. They exhibited a life of purity, holiness and self-denial. They exercised charity and benevolence, and they forced the respect of the surrounding pagans to a life the motives of which they could not comprehend, unless they resulted from principles higher than those their pagan religion afforded them ; and having won their respect for their lives and their gratitude for their benevolence, these monastic missionaries went among them with the Word of God in their hands, and preached to them the doctrines and pure morality of the Word of Life."

It is, of course, true that a Bishop, if a member of one of these monastic families, was subject, as such, to the rule and authority of the Abbot ; and it often happened, to avoid the restraint of Episcopal authority, that a monastery had its own Bishop, sometimes as Abbot, at other times as a member of the family. But there can be no question whatever as to the recognition of the Episcopate as a separate Order, both in its duties and its dignities. Moreover, the Bishops, and the Bishops *only,* ordained. When the Bishop celebrated the sacred mysteries, he broke the bread alone. And Adamnan records that on one occasion when a Bishop came to the monastery at Iona and did not make known his rank, that St. Columba was greatly distressed because, in ignorance of his office, due respect had not been paid to him. It follows, therefore, that no support whatever is given to the Presbyterian theory from the fact that the Abbot, even when only in priest's orders, was the head of the monastic family. Those families knew no such thing as parity of orders.

It is interesting to trace the work which the missionaries trained in Britain did for the Irish Church, and to compute the debt which Ireland owes to them. From what has been said already, it will be seen that to the British Church must be ascribed a very considerable share both in the founding and in the upbuilding of the Church in Ireland. But the ultimate results of its action were even greater than these. Monasticism supplied exactly what Ireland needed, and a most extraordinary outburst of zeal and enthusiasm followed. Ireland became the " Isle of Saints." Missionaries went forth from Ireland to all parts, as from the Holy Land in the first century of Christianity, when the Cross and the open tomb were yet fresh in the minds of men. She, too, had her Twelve Apostles, as Palestine had at an earlier period. Some nations, like China, have a long but comparatively barren life ; some, like England, develop slowly but continuously, and can produce successive harvests without impoverishing the soil ; others, like the State of Athens, have a sudden and splendid blossoming of youth and vigour, but it is brief and transient. Ireland belongs to the latter class. But she need not too bitterly bemoan her fortune. History, indeed, which extolled Athens, has neglected to do her justice, but this merely shews what bad

Christians we are, and how we still judge according to worldly and Pagan standards. "The glory of the celestial is one, and the glory of the terrestrial is another," and Ireland's glory was of the former class. Not only were her monasteries renowned far and wide for their learning, for their study of the arts, for their transcription of manuscripts, which were dispersed over Europe, and are still treasures in many a library, but they poured forth saints who carried to other lands the same burning zeal. It has been computed that thirteen monasteries were founded by the Irish in Scotland, twelve in England, seven in France, twelve in Armorica (Brittany), seven in Lorraine, ten in Alsatia, sixteen in Bavaria, fifteen in Rhetia, Helvetia and Allemania, besides others in Thuringia and on the left bank of the Lower Rhine, and six in Italy.

IRISH PATRONS OR FOUNDERS.

Of the saints of Irish origin, who are recognized as patrons or founders of churches, there were, it has been estimated, a hundred and fifty in Germany (of whom thirty-six were martyrs), forty-five in Gaul, thirty in Belgium, thirteen in Italy, and eight in Norway and Iceland.[1] Of all these saints two stand pre-eminent— *Columba* and *Columbanus*—who, from the similarity of their names, have often been confounded. Of *Columba* something has already been said. Of the other some account must also be given.

COLUMBANUS was born A.D. 543 (the year St. Benedict

---

[1] Montalambert, *Monks of the West*, Book IX., c. 8.

died), and was trained at the monastery of Bangor, near Belfast. He, with his missionary band, crossed into Gaul in 589, and establishing himself at the foot of the Vosges, amid relics of Roman greatness and Gaulish idolatry, he founded the great monastery of Luxeuil, also those of Anegray and Fontaines, into each of which he introduced the British custom of observing Easter.

After a residence of twenty years in the country he, having offended King Theodore, was driven from his court. He then went to Metz, and from thence into Switzerland, where he laboured for some time in the vicinity of Lake Zug. Afterwards he went into Italy, and in a gorge of the Appenines, not far from the site of Hannibal's victory of Trebbia, he founded the Abbey of Bobbio, which has been described as " the citadel of orthodoxy against the Arians, a focus of knowledge and instruction which was long the light of northern Italy."[1] Here he died in the year 615.

The monastery of Luxeuil became the founder of other monasteries, and for a time it seemed as if the stern rule of Columban would prevail over that of Benedict, and establish itself as the universal rule of the West.

It is evident from all this, that from an early period a strong missionary spirit pervaded the monasteries of Ireland and Scotland, and that before the coming of Augustine to Britain a remarkable body of missionaries went from Britain for the conversion of the continent.

[1] Montalambert, Vol. II., p. 438.

THE SAXONS NEGLECTED BY THE BRITISH CHURCH FOR A TIME. AT LAST SUCCESSFUL WORK BEGUN.

But famous as the British Church was in its missionary work abroad, it must be confessed that it entirely neglected work nearer home. It failed in not making efforts for the conversion of its Saxon neighbours, and so the field that it ought to have occupied was entered by Augustine, the foreigner. But when once aroused to a sense of its duty towards the Saxons we find its success in Pagan Britain as remarkable as it was praiseworthy. A small part only, as will be seen, of the Saxon kingdoms was converted to Christianity by missionaries from Rome ; by far the larger portion owes its conversion to missionaries of the native Church. Indeed, these native missionaries, for the most part, had a decided advantage over the missionaries of Augustine. They were trained in their own native monasteries, in the Saxon dialect, so that they could preach to the Saxons without the aid of interpreters ; but Augustine and his monks, not understanding the Saxon language, had to bring with them interpreters from Gaul. This was a serious drawback to Augustine, and a decided advantage to the British clergy.

St. Aidan. The great leader in the conversion of the Saxon kingdoms was *St. Aidan.* The late Bishop Lightfoot, of Durham, has well said[1] : " *Not Augustine, but Aidan, is the true Apostle of England.* ' From the cloisters of Lindisfarne (writes Montalambert) and from the heart of those districts, in which the popularity of

[1] Vide *Leaders in the Northern Church.* Sermon on " Celtic Missions of Iona and Lindisfarne."

ascetic pontiffs such as Aidan . . . took day by day a deeper root, Northumbrian Christianity spread over the Southern kingdoms. What is distinctly visible everywhere is the influence of Celtic priests and missionaries replacing and seconding Roman missionaries, and reaching districts which their predecessors had never been able to enter. Thus the stream of the Divine Word extended from North to South, and its slow but certain course reached in succession all the peoples of the Heptarchy.' And again, at the close of the chapter of which these are the opening words, he writes : ' Of the seven kingdoms of Anglo-Saxon Confederation, that of Kent alone was exclusively won and retained by the Roman monks, whose first attempts among the East Saxons and Northumbrians ended in failure. In Essex and in East Anglia the Saxons of the West and the Angles of the East were converted by the combined action of Continental missionaries and Celtic monks. As to the two Northumbrian kingdoms and those of Essex and Mercia, which comprehended in themselves more than two-thirds of the territory occupied by the German conquerors, these four countries owed their final conversion exclusively to the peaceful invasion of the Celtic monks, who not only rivalled the zeal of the Roman monks, but who, the first obstacles once surmounted, showed much more perseverance and gained much more success.' Sussex still remained—Sussex, the immediate neighbour of the Roman missionaries in Kent. Sussex was at length stormed and taken. And here again the conqueror of this last stronghold of heathendom, though an ardent champion of the Roman cause, was a Northumbrian by birth. *Wilfrid* had been a pupil of Aidan, and his missionary inspiration was drawn from Lindisfarne. Was I not right, then, in claiming for Aidan the first place in the evangelization of our race ? *Augustine was the Apostle of Kent*, but *Aidan was the Apostle of* ENGLAND."

THE CHURCH PLANETS OF BRITAIN.

A HYMN OF THE UNION OF THE ANCIENT CATHOLIC CHURCHES OF BRITAIN, AND THE CHURCHES COLONIAL AND AMERICAN.

The historic line of light here indicated is that which—following the scattered lights that came from the East and the West to ancient Britain—came from Scotland to Ireland by St. Patrick, from Ireland to Scotland by St. Columba, thence to Northumbria by St. Aidan, and thence, by his successors, throughout the Heptarchy of England, and was united with the light from Italy and Gaul by St. Augustine, and is now extended, in Catholic Unity, over the Asian, African, American and Australasian world.

As to some lordly mountain
   Which o'er a broad land reigns,
Or some full river's fountain
   Which feeds the far off plains,
When—praising God the Giver—
   Thy children's anthems rise,
Northumbria ! mount and river,
   To thee they lift their eyes.

Erin's Iona won thee—
   Isle of Saint Columb's cell—
Thence like new dawn upon thee
   His [1] prophet blessing fell :
Thence came his saintly Aidan,
   As with the full day's smile,
With Western treasure laden
   Eastward to [2] Holy Isle.

Kings made thy good their glory :
   They gave thee of their best ;

[1] Columba's dying prediction from the Torr Abb of Iona.

[2] Lindisfarne, off the Northumbrian coast.

All time shall tell the story
  Of Oswald and his [1] quest:
Of Hilda, in Christ's honour
  Won from her royal place,
Yet crowned with power upon her
  Of more than royal grace.

How sing of each light-leader
  Down all the radiant line?
Chad, Colman, Cuthbert, Beda,—
  With many a star they shine!
With Austin's constellation,
  And old [2] Saint David's flame—
They showed the One Salvation,
  So name them by one name!

O Sun of Truth and Glory,
  With these who shone by Thee
Shine [3] other spheres before Thee
  Past many a severing sea:
Each in his own course blessing
  Some far long-hidden land:
One Christ, one Creed confessing,
  Star-brethren of one band.

Praise to our God for ever
  Who these did call and send
Each to his own endeavour
  For one immortal end—
One Spiritual Nation
  'Neath one Eternal Sun,
The Church of our Salvation
  One in The Three-in-One! Amen.

S. J. STONE.

1 King Oswald sent to Iona for a Bishop to revive Christianity in Northumbria, after the flight of Paulinus. Aidan was finally sent.

2 The light of the ancient British Church in Wales was never quenched.

3 Asian, African, Australasian, American.

(By kind permission of the Rev. S. J. Stone and Messrs. Skeffington.)

CHAPTER IV.

THE MISSION OF AUGUSTINE.

GREGORY AND THE ROMAN SLAVE-MARKET—HIS RESOLVE TO PREACH THE GOSPEL TO THE ANGLES — PREVENTED FROM GOING — SENDS AUGUSTINE—THE TIME PROVIDENTIAL—ETHELBERT AND BERTHA— MEETS THE KING AT EBB'S FLEET—CORDIAL RECEPTION—SUCCESS FOLLOWS HIS PREACHING—CONSECRATED IN GAUL—MORE MISSION- ARIES SENT—PAGAN TEMPLES CONVERTED INTO CHRISTIAN CHURCHES —BRITISH MISSIONARIES JOIN HEARTILY IN THE WORK—LITURGY OF THE BRITISH CHURCH ; ITS EASTERN SOURCE—NOT THE SAME AS THAT USED AT ROME—THE BRITISH CHURCH, INDEPENDENT—RESISTS ATTEMPTS TO SECURE HER OBEDIENCE TO ROME—AUGUSTINE'S POLICY —CONFERENCES WITH THE BRITISH BISHOPS—AUGUSTINE'S PROPOSALS— THEIR ANSWER, BY DINOTH—AUGUSTINE, HIS FAULTS—HE EXTENDS THE WORK TO ROCHESTER AND LONDON—HIS DEATH AND BURIAL— CONCLUSION—HYMN TO THE CHURCH OF ENGLAND.

WE come now to speak of the arrival of Augustine, and of his mission in Britain. Gregory, after- wards Bishop of Rome, before his elevation to the Episcopate, chanced one day to be passing through the Roman slave-market, where he saw, among the slaves, some fair-complexioned, light-haired youths. Their fresh and beautiful countenances instantly at- tracted his attention. On inquiring whence they came, and who they were, he was told they were Angles, from Britain. "Ah !" replied Gregory, "they rather deserve the name of Angels." " From what province do they come ? " He was told they were from Deira, a district in Northumbria. "Deira," he said; "that is well—they are called to the mercy of God from His wrath *(de ira)*. But what is the name of the King of that province?" He was informed that it was Alla or Ælla—"Alleluia!" he exclaimed; "Alleluia must be sung to their country."

Influenced by these coincidences, Gregory resolved upon undertaking a mission into Britain, supposing that the inhabitants were all pagan. He would at once have carried this resolve into effect, had not his elevation to the Episcopate, in the year 590, prevented his leaving Rome. But the noble resolution of converting the Saxons was not abandoned, for immediately after his consecration he ordered a Gallic priest, named Candidus, to buy some Saxon youths, to be educated as missionaries for their native land.

The ardent mind of this prelate, however, could not endure the delay of educating missionaries for so pressing and darling an object. He resolved, therefore, on speedier measures. He looked around him for a man of zeal, talent, and resolution. Such an one he found ready for him, in the person of Augustine, the Prior of St. Andrew's. This enterprising ecclesiastic, having secured a band of forty monks as his associates, directed his course towards Britain; but on his way through Gaul his heart failed him, and he would have abandoned the undertaking had it not been for the rebuke of Gregory.

The time chosen was *providential*. Ethelbert, King of Kent, and Bretwalda over the other kingdoms of the Heptarchy (as we saw at p. 78), had married a Christian wife, Bertha, daughter of Charibert, King of Paris, on condition that she should be allowed the free exercise of her religion, and to take with her Luidhard, her chaplain. For her use a British church (St. Martin's, Canterbury) had been restored and made fit for service. Augustine, taking with him interpreters from France, came into Britain with singular advantages; he was the messenger of Gregory, whose spiritual power was widely acknowledged throughout Europe; he bore recommendations from the King of France, and was sure of the favour of Queen Bertha. Ethelbert, who no doubt already looked on Christianity with favour, was willing to receive the missionaries. They landed at Ebb's Fleet, on the island of Thanet, in A.D. 597—the same place where Hengist and Horsa landed a century and a half before—and after a few days delay the King proceeded to meet them. Augustine and his monks approached the King in formal procession. One bore on high a silver cross, another carried a banner with a representation of the Crucifixion of our Saviour, and all chanted a Litany. Through their interpreter they explained to the King the object of their mission. They told him they were come " to preach the word of life to him and to his people." " These are indeed fair words and promises which you bring with you," said the King, " but because they are new, and uncertain, I cannot at once take up with them, and leave the faith which I and the Saxon people have so long observed. But as you have come from far, and as I think you wish to give us a share in things which you believe to be true and most profitable, we will not show you unkindness, but rather will receive you hospitably, and not hinder you from converting as many as you can to your religion." This was all that they could expect. They were allowed to preach; they were also provided with sustenance, and given a temporary abode at Canterbury. They used St. Martin's church for their services; and by their preaching, as well as by their holy and self-denying lives, and their frequent prayers and fastings, they soon made many converts. Indeed the progress of the work of conversion was so great, and the success which crowned their efforts so extraordinary, that at Christmas of the same year Augustine and his associates are reported to have baptized 10,000 persons.

Soon afterwards the king declared himself a convert, and was baptized on the Whitsunday following, probably in St. Martin's Church.

The late *Archbishop Benson*, in a sermon preached at Perranzabuloe in 1878, when he was Bishop of Truro, said, " If St. Augustine had gone to Cornwall he would not have found there, as many perhaps might suppose, a multitude of heathen people; but there he would have found people holding the full knowledge of the Gospel, worshipping there day after day, as well as from Sunday to Sunday. St. Augustine [there] would have found himself amongst people who knew and loved the same Gospel which he taught."

Augustine, finding that so great a work had begun, saw the necessity of his obtaining Episcopal functions; so he repaired to Gaul, where he was *consecrated* in November, 597, by *Virgilius, Archbishop of Arles*, with the assistance of others, as " Archbishop of the English."

Returning to Britain he received from the king the gift of a palace for a residence, and met with such success that Gregory announced, in a letter to the Patriarch of Alexandria, that more than 10,000 Kentish men were baptized on Christmas Day (597).

In the spring of 598 Augustine sent two messengers, Lawrence, a priest, and Peter, a monk, to Rome, asking for additional help, and also the advice of Gregory as to the management of his new diocese. Augustine consulted him, too, as to the difference between the Roman and Gallican Liturgies, the latter of which was in use at St. Martin's, and by the British Church. Gregory told him to use whichever was most conducive to piety, and best suited to the English nation. In reply to another question, " How he was to deal with the Bishops of Gaul and Britain," Gregory gave him no authority over the former, but placed the latter under his jurisdiction.[1] He evidently thought that Augustine was established in London, which was to be one Metropolitan See, with twelve suffragan Bishops ; and York was selected as another, with twelve suffragans likewise. The two Metropolitans, after the death of Augustine, were to take precedence according to the priority of their consecration. Gregory sent him four other missionaries : Mellitus, Justus, Paulinus, and Ruffinianus, and with them he sent vestments for the clergy, and sacred vessels and ornaments for the Church,

---

[1] And yet Gregory professed reverence for the first four Councils: "Sicut quatuor Evangelii libros, sic quatuor concilia venerari me fateor." In the 8th Canon of the Council of Ephesus the principle, which, from its relating to the Church in Cyprus, in the first instance, is known as the "*Jus Cyprium*," is laid down that "no Bishop shall occupy another province which has not been subject to him from the beginning."

with some relics of Apostles and martyrs, and a few books. He sent him the pall also.

The little church of St. Martin was soon found too small for the increasing converts. Gregory had advised Augustine to consecrate the heathen temples, and turn them into Christian churches; so he recovered from heathen uses, and re-consecrated, an old British Church which stood a ruin near his palace. This church was on the spot *where now stands Canterbury Cathedral.* Between this and St. Martin's stood what had once been another British Church. This also he re-dedicated; and here he laid the foundation of the great monastery of SS. Peter and Paul, which, after a time, took the name of St. Augustine. On this site, so much of the ancient structure as possible being retained, was built, A.D. 1844, the noble *College of St. Augustine's*, with a view to carrying out the purpose that SS. Gregory and Augustine had so much at heart, the education of missionaries for foreign work. One of the pagan temples, too, was converted into a Christian church and dedicated to St. Pancras.[1]

Thus far all was done with the excellent motive of conciliating the British people. The next step which Augustine took, however, was calculated to disgust them. If Gregory had realized that the British Church, wasted as it was with persecution, enjoyed a claim of Apostolical foundation equal to his own, he would not

---

[1] It is not a little singular that the last Church in England that refused to throw off the Roman usages at the Reformation was St. Pancras in London. And it is a lamentable fact that at the end of twenty years almost all of those converted through Augustine's instrumentality had lapsed again into their former superstitions.

probably have forgotten his controversy with John the Faster, and the Ephesine Canon, and placed a primitive and independent Church under the jurisdiction of Augustine. The latter appears to have discovered at last that there was a British Church, and that there were British Bishops, who ought to be considered. We have dwelt on the successful efforts of these Roman missionaries hitherto, and of the happy combination of events which led to their favourable reception by the Saxons. It must not be supposed, however, that whilst Augustine and his associates were occupied in evangelizing the Saxons the British Christians took no part in the work. Although that Church had been heavily oppressed and weakened by the persecution of the Saxon conquerors, who had driven her Bishops out of the land, and caused them to take refuge in Wales and Cornwall, yet it was not destroyed—the flame of pure Christianity burned in many an obscure corner, and many a British priest emerged from the deep glens and forests, and, like St. John in the wilderness, with no better fare than locusts and wild honey, proclaimed the joyful tidings of the Gospel in that dark day of misery and gloom. Among the most celebrated of these noble confessors were Kentigern, St. Asaph, and St. Columba, men who hazarded their lives in those perilous times; and through their instrumentality numbers of Saxons abandoned their idolatrous worship (just as the Druids had previously done) and embraced Christianity. The gross delusion that Romanists would palm upon the world, that to Augustine and his missionaries belong the entire glory of Britain's conversion, is not only absolutely false with regard to the Britons, but it is not true even with respect to the Saxons. This fact ought to be borne in mind, because it not only shows that the British Church existed as a distinct and independent Church at the time of Augustine's arrival, but also that she possessed sufficient strength and vitality to extend the curtains of her tent, even in the hour of her heaviest oppression ; and notwithstanding all Augustine's endeavours, through wealth, power, and intrigue, to establish an authority over her (as we shall presently see), yet she maintained her dignified position ; and from the mountains of Wales and Cornwall, the fens of Somersetshire, and the forests of Northumbria, " she set up her banners for tokens " of uncompromising independence.

LITURGY.

Let us pause for a moment to ascertain what Liturgy the British Church was using, and from what source it had been derived.

Aristobulus being a Greek, and a disciple of St. Paul, would, naturally, when he went to Britain, carry with him the ecclesiastical rites of the Eastern Churches, and this accounts in part for the correspondence between the Eastern and the British rites at that time.

Here let it be remembered that there were still existing four great Liturgies, which had come down from the primitive times, and were the original sources from which all others were derived. These were known as the Liturgies of St. James, St. John, St. Peter, and St. Mark, and from their origin in the first age of the faith were, of course, similar in their general features. The Liturgy of St. John was used not only in the East, by the Ephesine Church, but also in Western Europe; and from the Gallican Church the Christians in Britain received it. Such was the testimony of tradition among those by whom it had been adopted.

The ancient author, whose tract has been published by Spelman, and who is allowed by all critics not to have written later than the beginning of the eighth century, thus positively affirms that " John the Evangelist first chanted the Gallican course, then afterwards the blessed Polycarp, disciple of St. John, and then, thirdly, Irenæus, who was Bishop of Lyons in Gaul, chanted the same course in Gaul." [1]

The Church of Rome was using the Liturgy of St. Peter, which differed in some particulars from that of St. John which other Western Churches had adopted. We may learn this from the celebrated letter (already referred to) written to Gregory by Augustine, in which the latter asks for advice touching certain points of inquiry. One question was, what course he ought to pursue in reference to the Gallican Liturgy, which, though different from the Roman, was in use in the British and Gallic Churches.[2] In reply, Gregory told him that he had nothing to do with the Bishops of Gaul, who were subject to the Bishop of Arles as their Metropolitan; that he ought to have authority over the British Bishops; and that, in reference to the Liturgy, he ought to adopt that which would be most acceptable to the Saxon Church.[3]

[1] Spelman, *Concilia*, Tom. I., p. 176.   [2] Bede, *Eccles. Hist.*, lib. I., c. 21.
[3] Ibid, I. 27.

From whence he derived the right thus to give Augustine authority over an independent Church it would be difficult to show.

Three facts are here conclusively established : (1) That there were canonical and lawful Bishops in Britain before Augustine went there. Consequently, he owed submission to the Metropolitan of Britain, according to the then existing canons of the Church ; (2) That the Liturgy used in Gaul was not the same as the Roman ; (3) That this Liturgy was used in Britain. And, as we have seen already, it was the Ephesine, the Liturgy of St. John. It is therefore evident that the British Church did not derive her *Liturgy* from Rome ; neither did she, even through Augustine, receive her *Orders* from that Church.

INDEPENDENCE.

This brings us to a most important epoch in the history, not only of the British Church in particular, but of the Christian Church in general, viz., the time when the Roman Pontiffs began to unfurl the banner of universal dominion, and to set at naught the power of princes. The mission of Augustine, by whatever motive undertaken, was the point of the papal wedge, which, first insinuated into the body ecclesiastical of England, by Gregory, was by his successors driven deeper and deeper, until at length, by Pope Innocent III., in the thirteenth century, it effectually destroyed (thank God only for a time) the independence of the British Church.

Gregory's views with regard to Britain were of an ambitious character. And the success which had attended the mission of Augustine excited in him an ardent longing for jurisdiction over the Church in Britain. Augustine, understanding well the love of his master for the marvellous, regaled him with an account of the miraculous incidents of his work. Gregory implicitly believed it all.

We have seen above that Gregory, in his letter of instruction to Augustine, told him that he " ought to have authority over the British Bishops." Speedily responding to his instructions, Augustine began seriously to apply himself to the reduction of the whole British Church to the obedience of Rome. But he strangely miscalculated the pliancy of the British character, and little understood the actual state of religion among the people. Fuller, the Church historian, says that on his arrival " Augustine found a plain religion (simplicity is a badge of antiquity) practised by the Britons ; some of whom were living in the contempt, and many others in ignorance, of worldly vanities. He brought in a religion, spun with a coarser thread, though guarded with a finer trimming, made luscious to the senses with pleasing ceremonies, so that many who could not judge of the goodness were attracted by the gaudiness thereof." And again, the same author testifies that the poor " Christian Bishops living peaceably at home, enjoyed God, the Gospel, and their mountains ; little skilful in, and less caring for the ceremonies (*à la mode*) brought over by Augustine ; and, indeed, their poverty, which could not go to the cost of Augustine's silver cross, made them worship the God of their fathers after their own homely but hearty fashion ; not willing to disturb Augustine and his followers in their *new rites*, but that *he* had a mind to disquiet them in their *old Service,* as the sequel shows."

How beautiful this picture drawn by the historian, of the simple, unpretending, and tolerant religion of our ancient Church ! How strikingly it contrasts with the ostentatious and heartless pageantry of those " new rites " which were now forced upon her !

The policy of Augustine was to undermine this simplicity of worship among the Britons, and to work upon the imaginations of the wonder-loving Saxons by means of that gaudy ritual, and those enticing doctrines, which he imported from Italy. The worship of images, the flames of purgatory, the efficacy of good works for the attainment of salvation, the virtue of relics, were among the ready instruments which he employed. Augustine's austerity of manner, and sanctity of deportment, effectually secured the veneration of many. Gregory was transported with joy on hearing of the continued prosperity of the mission, and, in a letter to Ethelbert, he exhorted him to assist " Augustine in his good work by all the expedients of exhortation, *terror, and correction.*"

How soon the Church of Rome exhibited her tender mercies of " *terror and correction* " towards the inhabitants of Britain ! Is it any wonder that though a large number of his Saxon subjects nominally embraced Christianity during the life-time of Ethelbert, after his death nearly all of them lapsed into their former idolatry, from which many of them were reclaimed by Augustine's successors ? Notwithstanding all Augustine's efforts to bow the necks of British Christians to receive the yoke of a foreign power, the Britons, amidst all their wrongs and sufferings, adhered rigidly to the customs of their forefathers, and showed no disposition to surrender their independence. So far from acknowledging the authority of the Pope over them, they had never before heard that he claimed any, and, therefore, they resolved to maintain their independence. This resolution Augustine determined to counteract, and though he did not even pretend to have authority from Gregory for his acts, yet he resolved if possible to reduce the Britons to submission.

To this end he convened a Synod of British Bishops (A.D. 602), at which he proposed a scheme for conformity to the Church of Rome, and, to make sure of his aim, dealt unsparingly in promises. The Venerable Bede, however, assures us (and his authority as a Saxon on this point will not be questioned) "*that the demands of Augustine were at once rejected, and all foreign jurisdiction over their Church was repelled by the unanimous voice of the assembled Bishops.*" [1]

We have already said that Saxon oppression and tyranny had driven the British Prelates into Wales, Cornwall, and other mountainous parts of the island. There, in greater security, they regulated their own ecclesiastical affairs, educated young men for the ministry, and watched with painful solicitude the movements of the Roman missionaries. The Metropolitan Church, for greater security, had already been removed from Caerleon to Llandaff, and thence to St. David's—

---

[1] Bede, *Eccles. Hist.*, Lib. II., c. 2. Edit. Cant., fol.

so called from the holy and venerable man who first presided over that See.

To these Cambrian (or Welsh) confines Augustine directed his steps, and convened a second Synod at a place called St. Augustine's Oak, near the banks of the Severn. At this Synod *seven* British Bishops were present, together with Dinoth, the learned and spirited abbot of Bangor, and several learned men, chiefly from the monastery of Bangor-Iscoed.

On their way to the conference these pious representatives consulted a hermit, renowned for his wisdom, as to whether they should forsake their traditions and yield to Augustine. The recluse said, " If he be a man of God take his advice." But how were they to know this, they asked. " That," said the hermit, "is no difficult matter. Contrive to be last in reaching the conference. If Augustine show humility and rise at your approach, be sure he is a true servant of the humble-minded Jesus; but if he receive you sitting, and show pride, he is not a man of God, maintain your ancient usages." This was an unfortunate test for the haughty monk, whose pride was gratified by the popular admiration for him. The Britons advanced. Their dignified and venerable appearance won the respect of the assembled multitude. Augustine did not condescend to rise, but he addressed them in the same unconciliatory manner as before. " In many things," he said, " you act contrary to our customs, and indeed to those of the universal Church, yet, if you will obey me in these three things: (1) to celebrate Easter at the proper time; (2) to perform the Office of Baptism, in which we are born again to God, according to the custom of the Holy Roman Church; and (3) join with us in preaching the Word of God to the English nation, *we will tolerate all your other customs though contrary to our own.*"   It is to be observed that these are matters of discipline only; that Augustine charges the British Bishops with no difference from Rome in doctrine; nay, if they had held false doctrine, he would not have asked them to join him in preaching to the English.

The British Bishops, disgusted with his discourtesy, resolved that they would utterly refuse submission to the Church of Rome and to Augustine.   Dinoth, in the name of the British Bishops,[1] made the following reply—

" Be it known, and without doubt, unto you, that we all are, and every one of us, obedient subjects to the Church of God, and to the Bishop of Rome, and to every godly Christian, to love every one in his degree in perfect charity, and to help all of them, by word and deed, to be the children of God: and other obedience than this I do not know to be due to him whom you call Pope, nor do I know the title Father of Fathers to be claimed or demanded; and this obedience we are ready to give, and to pay to him, and to every Christian continually.   *Besides, we are under the government of the Bishop of Caerleon-upon-Usk,*[2] *who is to oversee under God over us, to cause us to keep the way spiritual.*"[3]

[1] According to Welsh tradition, these are the Bishops who disputed with Augustine, viz. :—(1) The Bishop of Caerfawydd, called Hereford; (2) The Bishop of Teilo, *i.e.*, Llandaff; (3) The Bishop of Llanbadarn Fawr; (4) The Bishop of Bangor; (5) The Bishop of Llanelwy (St. Asaph); (6) The Bishop of Wegg; (7) The Bishop of Morganwg.   (Haddan and Stubbs, Vol. III., 41.)

[2] The Metropolitan See, which had been at Caerleon, had been transferred to St. David's, so that it was called by both titles indifferently.

[3] Copied from an ancient British MS. by Sir Henry Spelman.

A protest so bold, direct, and uncompromising, little suited the temper of Augustine, who had before shewn great want of discretion, but who now showed an equal want of what for missionary work is all important, good temper and charity. He left the Bishops with a prophecy, or, as Bede calls it, a threat—" Since you will not have peace with your brethren, you will have war with your enemies ; and if you will not preach the way of life to the English nation, you will suffer at their hands the vengeance of death." These words had a terrible fulfilment. They proved to be but too prophetic of impending slaughter. Bede says, " All of which fell out exactly as he had predicted." Augustine now addressed himself to the Saxons, and by working upon their superstitious attachment to himself and the Roman See, prevailed upon them to aid him in the subjugation of the British Church. He found in Ethelfrid, king of Northumbria, a suitable instrument for his purpose, for at the instigation of that disappointed monk, this prince attacked the Britons at Chester, A.D., 613.[1] On the battlefield were a large body of priests from the neighbouring monastery of Bangor-Iscoed (2,000), totally unarmed, for the purpose of encouraging, by their prayers and exhortations, the spirits of their brave defenders.[2] Ethelfrid, fearing no doubt the efficacy of this mode of encouragement, told his soldiers that whilst " those men fought with *prayers*, they fought with the sword." He then ordered his soldiers to

[1] Hore, in his *Eighteen Centuries*, says, " Of this Augustine, who had been dead eight years when it occurred, must have been entirely innocent."

[2] Bede, *Hist. Eccl. Angl.*, lib. I., c. 27.

attack them, which they accordingly did, and the British clergy were put to a dreadful slaughter, no fewer than 1,200 of them being killed.[1]

Whether Augustine was or was not the instigator of this cold-blooded murder of helpless priests, he certainly bore the blame of it, and entailed on himself and the Romish missionaries the distrust of every Briton. Had he possessed more humility, and greater suavity of disposition, his name might have passed down to posterity with greater honour; but whatever share of praise is due to him for his efforts to evangelize the Saxons, the British Church could regard him only with fear and distrust; and we, looking in retrospect at his character through the vista of thirteen centuries, cannot close our eyes to that haughty intolerance with which he vainly attempted the utter subjection of the British Church. Fuller says, "We commend his pains, condemn his pride, allow his life, approve his learning . . . and admit the foundation of his doctrines—*Jesus Christ*—but refuse the *wood, hay, and stubble* which he built thereupon."[2]

On his return to Canterbury, after these Conferences, he was able to add to the work which he had begun. The diocese of ROCHESTER was founded, Ethelbert having built a church there, which Augustine dedicated to St. Andrew, in remembrance of his abbey at Rome. The charge of the new See was committed to Justus.

Sebert, King of Essex, was the son of Ethelbert's sister, Ricula. He was persuaded by Augustine to

---

[1] Selden on Polyolb., 186. Also, Hore's *Eighteen Centuries*, p. 70.
[2] *Church History*, B. II., p. 68.

embrace Christianity, and then Mellitus was appointed Bishop of London, the capital of the kingdom. Ethelbert, with the assistance of Sebert, his nephew, built the Cathedral of St. Paul (known as East Minster), on the site which had for many years been occupied by the Temple of *Diana*. Another church was erected on Thorney Island, and by way of distinction it was called West Minster. It was reared on the site of the Temple of *Apollo*.

Augustine departed this life in the year 604, and was buried in the churchyard of his then unfinished monastery.[1] It must be confessed that he was not a successful missionary. He was lacking in those qualities which are absolutely essential for mission work—courage, good temper, discretion, and large-heartedness. Under peculiarly favourable circumstances, the soil being well prepared for him, he had effected the conversion of the kingdom of Kent, he had founded two bishoprics in that county, and had established also the See of London. This was far from realizing the scheme pointed out to him by Gregory. Moreover, he had done irreparable harm, by laying the foundation of a long-continued ill-feeling between the British and the Anglo-Saxon Churches.[2]

[1] The monastery was consecrated by his successor, Lawrence, who transferred the remains of Augustine to a grave in the northern part of the church. In 1091 his body was removed to Canterbury Cathedral.

[2] It is a little curious that *the Church of Wales* (*i.e.*, the survival of the old British Church) retained its independence down to A.D. 1115. Then was effected a union of the Welsh and Anglo-Saxon (or English) Churches, and the old British Church acknowledged the supremacy of Canterbury. The union of the British and Anglo-Saxon Churches prepared the way for the union of the country of Wales with the English realm. There had been for some time an interchange of friendly offices between these Churches, as when a Bishop of St. David's did the work of an infirm Bishop of Hereford before the Conquest; and a Bishop of Bangor had been translated to the See of Ely. *Vide* Lane's *Illustrated Notes on Eng. Ch. Hist.*, p. 174.

But we acknowledge a debt of gratitude which England owes to him. He renewed the union of the kingdom, which Hengist had destroyed. The *new* England was admitted into the older Commonwealth of nations; the civilization, arts, letters, which had fled before the sword of the English conquest, returned with the Christian Faith.

At his death the work of evangelizing England (of which he can be considered only as the pioneer) had just begun. Only two kingdoms of the Heptarchy, Kent and Essex (and these soon relapsed into paganism), had been reached by his teaching. His failure was fatal to all hope of England's conversion from Rome.[1] And, as we have already seen, the native Church was the chief agent in the work which it had so long and so inexcusably neglected.[2]

CONCLUSION.

The proof, then, is complete that the British is an ancient and Apostolic Church, independent of all foreign jurisdiction, and totally distinct from the Church of Rome which Augustine tried to introduce as a supplanter. By a reference to dates it will be seen that she was

[1] Hore's *Eighteen Centuries*, pp. 71, 72.

[2] This statement is so true, that 63 years after the landing of Augustine, *i.e.*, in A.D. 660, when all the Heptarchy, except Sussex, had been converted, *Wini*, Bishop of Winchester, was the only Bishop of the Romish Communion in Britain, and he had purchased his first Bishopric of London from Wulfhere, King of Mercia: all the rest were British. The cause is evident: *Patrick*, the Apostle of Ireland; *Ninian*, the Apostle of the Southern Picts; *Aidan*, of the Northumbrians; *Paul Hên*, his successor; *Columba*, of the Scotch; *Finan*, of the East Angles; *Chad*, of the Mercians, were all native Britons, and educated in the native colleges. The Romish succession had died down to one prelate, and Saxon Christianity was kept alive or refounded by British Christians. Vide *St. Paul in Britain*, Morgan. Note, pp. 184, 185.

I

planted in that island at least 400 years before the Saxon invasion, and nearly 550 years before the arrival of Augustine. That she was publicly recognized by the government of the country 146 years before the Church of Rome was so acknowledged on the banks of the Tiber. That from the first moment of her existence, to the days of Gregory the Great, the Bishops of Rome neither claimed nor received her submission. Indeed, popery, as a tyrannical power, assuming supremacy and infallibility, was at that time unknown, and continued unknown till the pontificate of Boniface, A.D. 606. He assumed a supremacy, but in a mild form when compared with the arrogant claims of some of his successors. So that for the first six centuries of Christianity we look in vain for any resemblance to that Church, which, in the after ages, "lorded it over God's heritage," and whose Bishop still claims to be "Universal Bishop" and "Infallible"—"Christ's Vicar on the earth."

Surely "to know that the Church of Britain was coeval with the age of the Apostles, is to build our faith on grounds most solid and interesting. But to extend that proof to the individual labours of one of the Apostles, and to find ourselves indebted for the first knowledge of the greatest blessings ever conferred on mankind to the personal zeal of the great Apostle of the Gentiles; and, in this search after truth, to find further, that the father of a British prince was instrumental in the first introduction of the Gospel into Britain; that it was publicly professed and protected by a British king, before the end of the second century; that a

British king was the first Christian prince of any land ; that Christianity was established throughout the Roman Empire by a native Briton ; these considerations, while they greatly increase our interest in the belief and service of Christianity, and augment our responsibility, may justly lead us to adopt the language of Moses— ' What nation is there so great, which hath God so nigh unto them, as the Lord our God is in all things that we call upon Him for ; and what nation is there so great, that hath statutes and judgments so righteous '— a religion so pure, a Church so Apostolic, a polity so wise and equitable, and blessings so ample and so various, as God hath bestowed upon this our favoured country ? " [1]

HYMN OF THE CHURCH OF ENGLAND.

O Church of our fathers in England,
  O Home of the Living Lord,
Full Fountain of Faith for ages,
  And Witness firm to the word
From Alban, Augustine, and Aidan,
  Paulinus, and Cuthbert, and Bede,
To our days, even ours, what armies
  Of Christ His long triumph lead !

Saints, known to Him only in Heaven,
  Or famed in their own despite ;
Or spending and spent for others,
  Or crown'd with the martyr-light ;
Of whom the world was not worthy,
  Who counted earth's riches as dross ;
They are resting in God's own acre,
  Their bed 'neath the Saving Cross.

[1] Bishop of St. David's, *Tracts*, p. 144.

The sin-defaced offspring of Adam,
  While centuries onward glide,
Have grown in the field of England:
  The tares with the wheat beside :
O visible fold of the Shepherd,
  How oft in His sorrow surveyed,
As the myriad snares of Satan
  His cause have again betrayed !

The Presence unseen at the altar,
  The Fountain of heav'nly Birth,
The gifts of the Holy Spirit
  Abide with the Church upon earth ;
While, heavenward high, the cathedral,
  O'er sin-strife and turmoil below,
Lifts the Sign of the great forgiveness
  The peace which the world cannot know.

Nor stand we alone in Thy mercy,
  Nor only beloved are we ;
For sheep of another folding
  Are secretly known unto Thee :
Grace-led while unknowingly straying,
  Or stumbling in sceptical gloom,
While the glare of the Present effaces
  The Cross and the vacant Tomb.

What then, if in ignorant anger,
  Or doing they know not what,
Or casting, in strange alliance,
  With infidel legions their lot,
The foes of the Faith in its beauty
  The Church of our fathers would smite !
Not in strength of our own, O Saviour,
  We gird for the sacred fight.

All wrongfulness, firm yet forgiving,
  O brothers, in faith endure;
Yet fight for the Lord's own dower,
  The heritage left to His poor.
Though spoilers are raging around us,
  We stand with full trust in His word;
For our house on the Rock is founded,
  The Rock of the Living Lord.

O Boat on Gennesareth heaving,
  Though storm-rack and wind assail,
We know that the powers of darkness
  Shall never against thee prevail.
The Holy One moves in the tempest,
  The storm-cries of fury are stay'd,
And the voice of our Captain cheers us,
  "Tis I ; be ye not afraid."   Amen.

F. T. PALGRAVE,
Prof. of Poetry in the University of Oxford.

THE SETTLEMENT AND CONVERSION OF THE HEPTARCHY.

Tribe and Leader.	Name of Kingdom.	Date of Occupation. A.D.	Date of Conversion. A.D.	First Bishop, and Source from which their Episcopal Succession was derived.
Jutes. Hengist and Horsa	Kent ...	449	597	1. *Augustine*, from *Rome*. Consecrated in Gaul.
	Sussex ...	477	681	2. *Wilfrid*, a monk of *Lindisfarne*, who afterwards became a strong partisan of the Italians. Consecrated in Gaul.
Saxons. Ælle	Wessex ...	495	634	3. *Birinus*, from *Rome*. Consecrated in Gaul.
Cissa ... ... Cerdic and Cynric	Essex ...	530	654	4. *Cedd*, from *Lindisfarne*. Mellitus of Rome established himself among them in 603, but his converts lapsed back to paganism in 616. Consecrated by Celtic Bishops.
	Northumbria	547	635	5. *Aidan*, from *Iona*. Paulinus of Rome went to Northumbria in 626, but his work was destroyed by the pagans in 633. Consecrated by Celtic Bishops.
Angles.	Mercia ...	560	653	6. *Diuma*, a Monk from *Lindisfarne*. Consecrated by Celtic Bishops.
Ida	East Anglia...	585	631	7. *Felix*, a Bishop of *Burgundy*, and *Fursey*, a monk of *Ireland*. The Roman Missionaries had previously made two unsuccessful attempts to plant Christianity in these provinces.

Ancient Dioceses.	First Bishop.	Date of Foundation.	Remarks.
		A.D.	
Armagh	St. Patrick ...	432	Trained most likely by St. German and St. Martin.
Llandaff	Dubricius ...	500	Became Archbishop of Caer-le-on.
St. David's ...	St. David ...	540	Consecrated by the Patriarch of Jerusalem.
Bangor	St. Daniel ...	516	Founded by the brethren of the College of the same name.
St. Asaph... ...	St. Kentigern ...	560	Owes its establishment to St. Kentigern.

Famous Monasteries.	Noted Priors or Abbots.	Date of Foundation.	Remarks.
		A.D.	
Iona	St. Columba ...	566	A pupil of St. Finnian, &c., once Abbot of Durrough.
Lindisfarne ...	St. Aidan ...	635	A Monk of Iona—Founder and Bishop.
	St. Cuthbert ...		Became Prior of Landisfarne.
Melrose	St. Cuthbert ...	651	Branch from Landisfarne—Cuthbert its first Abbot.

It follows from the foregoing that Lindisfarne was founded from Iona, and Melrose from Lindisfarne. *St. Aidan*, a Monk from Iona, founded Lindisfarne, and was its first Abbot. He was a Bishop. St. Cuthbert (a Brother) became Prior of Melrose. He was afterwards sent to Lindisfarne, where he became its Prior.

If it is fair to suppose that the coming of Augustine from Rome, when only a monk in priests' orders, is equivalent to the establishment of an Italian hierarchy in England, it is no less reasonable to argue that Theodore's selection of monks belonging to the monasteries founded by the old British Church, to be Bishops among the Anglo-Saxons, was equally a continuance of the ancient Christianity of Britain. Henceforth there was a double line of Apostolic Ministry in the Anglo-Saxon Church; and when by degrees the Scottish, Irish and British (*i.e.* Welsh) Churches agreed to recognize the primacy of the Archbishop of Canterbury[1] (always understanding that this did not include any right of the Pope of Rome to interfere with their affairs), this double succession was further strengthened, nay, rather it was made a *threefold cord* through the consecration of St. David by the Patriarch of Jerusalem.

[1] The Church in Wales did not recognize the primacy of the Archbishop of Canterbury till the year A.D. 1115. Then took place a union between the Welsh and the English Churches, which prepared the way for the union of Wales with England.